# Imparting The Blessing

# Study Guide

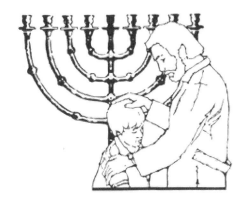

# 8 Weeks Program

## To

# Understand and Practice

## Imparting Blessing

## &

## Breaking the Verbal Curse

**Web: thefathersblessing.com**

The Father's Blessing Study Guide
Copyright by William T. Ligon Sr.

Published by The Father's Blessing
P.O. Box 1218
Brunswick, GA 31521

# Weekly Lesson Plan
# &
# Table Of Contents

**Please read Lesson 1 & 2 before attending the first weeks class.**

Read each lesson and perform their assignments before attending that weeks class. Example: read **Lessons 3& 4** before attending class **Week 2**, and so on.

Begin planning your "Blessing Service" at the Week 6 gathering as to its location, whether or not you will have a meal, and whether you will have any other special guest or preparations.

Note: **Week 6 = Lesson 11 & Week 7 = Lesson 10**
Please show the DVD lessons accordingly.

# Lesson 1

Welcome to the exciting world of biblical blessings. You are about to begin a journey that will release the favor of God into many areas of your life. Commitment to complete this eight weeks study will insure that God's plan of releasing blessings on your life and the lives of your family members will become a reality.

Both the Old Testament and the New Testament are full of evidence that God intends for the spoken blessing to be used to impart favor to His people. Quotes from the teachings of Jesus as well as statements from Paul and Peter support the use of the spoken blessing as a way of breaking a curse over oneself and enjoying the protection of God against the curse. Further evidence reveals that parental blessings spoken over children produce positive results in the lives of the children. These same positive results can be fully experienced by adults who have long ago left home and may or may not have parents who are living. Every single person on this side of eternity, with God's grace, can come to an understanding of the principals of blessing and apply them to his or her benefit.

### It should be noted

The New Testament distinguishes between **two types** of blessings and two types of curses.

The first refers to **the curse of the Law and the blessing of Abraham**. It expresses the glorious mercy that the curse of sin, resulting in eternal damnation, has been broken by the crucifixion of Jesus Christ on the cross. It is found in Galatians 3:13-14 which says:

**Gal 3:13-14 (KJV)**
**13 Christ hath redeemed us from the curse of the law, being made a curse for us: for it is written, Cursed is every one that hangeth on a tree: 14 That the blessing of Abraham might come on the Gentiles through Jesus Christ; that we might receive the promise of the Spirit through faith.**
**KJV**

The second is **the spoken blessing and the spoken curse** (malediction) which deals with the words that people speak to each other or about each other.

**1 Peter 3:8,9 (KJV)**
**8 Finally, be ye all of one mind, having compassion one of another, love as brethren, be pitiful, be courteous: 9 Not rendering evil for evil, or railing for railing: but contrariwise blessing; knowing that ye are thereunto called, that ye should inherit blessing.**
**KJV**

**The Lord has provided a way to impart His favor and break the power of curses that have been spoken over us. It is verbal blessings.**

A brief look at the blessing of Abraham and Curse of the Law is included for clarity and to help fortify faith for the participants of verbal blessings. The spoken blessing will be our main focus with the purpose of creating an atmosphere, first in the share groups and then in the homes, **where children and adults can give and receive spoken blessings and harvest the benefits of those blessings in their lives.** When one examines the institution of the High Priestly Blessing in the Old Testament (Numbers 6:23-27 and Leviticus 9:22-23), it becomes evident that God instituted it as a **spoken blessing** to impart special grace to His people. Passages in the New Testament come alive with meaning when studied in the light of the Old Testament spoken blessings. May the Lord Himself bless you as you study His word concerning blessing, that your understanding will be opened and that you will be stirred to action springing from the knowledge of this Biblical truth.

## God has placed great power in the spoken blessing.

**Of the two types of blessings and curses, this workbook focuses on the spoken blessing and the spoken curse.**

# Welcome From The Ligons

We welcome you to the eight weeks (twelve lesson) program designed to lead families into the practice of imparting to each other the blessings of the Lord. You are beginning a journey to build strong healthy relationships among your family members. As you learn to give and receive blessing, you will enjoy the favor of the Lord in many areas of your life. God Himself established this plan as His way of releasing His favor and blessings upon His children. It is not something new. The fact is, it is as old as the creation of man--for God's first act after creating Adam and Eve was to speak a blessing over them.

**(Genesis 1:28) (KJV)**

**28 And God blessed them, and <u>God said unto them</u>, Be fruitful, and multiply, and replenish the earth, and subdue it: and have dominion over the fish of the sea, and over the fowl of the air, and over every living thing that moveth upon the earth.**

## Your Goals For Your Family

_____
_____
_____
_____
_____
_____

## The Father's Blessing Goals

1. To train and establish families in a practice of imparting the blessing as a way of life.
2. To teach them to use the resources God has provided to bring health and life into their homes.

## Your Anticipated Results For your Family

_____
_____
_____
_____
_____
_____
_____

## Our Anticipated Results

1. A release of God's favor upon each family member who practices blessing and upon each one who receives blessing.
2. Protection given to those who have been laboring under spoken curses that have been spoken against them.
3. New and exciting opportunities will open up to those who take the High Priestly Blessing seriously.

## Each Believer is a Priest of God

The apostle Peter identified each believer as a priest of God when he wrote, *"But you are a chosen generation, a royal priesthood...* (I Peter 2:9a KJV). According to I Peter 1:2a he was writing to the *"elect according to the fore knowledge of God the Father..."* Those believers, he wrote, were called to *"not render (-ing) evil for evil, or railing for railing; but contrariwise blessing, knowing that ye are there unto called, that ye should inherit a blessing. "* (I Peter 3:9 KJV).

We have been teaching the principles of blessing since 1974. Letters have been received from families who practice the blessing daily in their homes indicating they see the favor of the Lord come upon their family members when they put the principles into practice on a daily basis.

## Our Concern

Our concern has been that the majority of people often sit through a series of teachings at their church without making any effort to apply what they have heard to their lives. Thus, they miss the blessings promised to those who will do what the Lord has commanded. That is why we now offer the eight weeks (twelve lesson) plan of Blessing. We are confident that families who devote eight weeks of concentrated effort to learning the principles of blessing will continue the practice after the classes are over. Many of the families will be challenged to enlist other families to study the program with them.

## Congratulations

<u>We want to personally congratulate you for being concerned enough about your family and home to dedicate this time to the program.</u> We are so pleased to have you join the growing list of blessing families and look forward to a long, exciting time together.

## Consider Leading a Group

During the eight weeks of your family study with the other families in your group, consider the possibility of becoming a TORCHBEARER FAMILY. Torchbearers give leadership to other families by leading a group of families in the study and practice of blessing principles. Torchbearers were people who carried portable lights on poles consisting of a long piece of resinous wood or twisted tow dipped in tallow, flaming at one end. <u>The light gave illumination to others to see clearly where to travel</u>. Torchbearers have been used in Olympic Games where the torch became the symbol of excellence.

## The Fruit

Spiritually, a TORCHBEARER brings enlightenment and inspiration to biblical truths. As Torchbearers, you will have the rewarding experience of seeing other families enter into the blessings and favor of God. Old destructive habits will be dissolved as the families learn new ways of receiving from God and giving His loving favor away to others.

## Where to Begin

The steps into Torchbearers leadership are:

(1) **Blessing Family:** Become a Blessing Family by enrolling in and completing the eight weeks program of study.

(2) **Journeyman Family:** Commit to become an assistant family with a Torchbearer family. As a Journeyman Family, you will help lead and teach a new class.

(3) **Torchbearer Family:** Having completed the course yourselves and trained the second time by helping to lead, you now take the leadership of a new group with a Journeyman family assisting you. The family who moves into Torchbearer leadership will experience the greatest benefits from the course. Preparing to teach and leading other into better understanding of Biblical truths opens up our lives to dynamic spiritual growth.

# How It All Began

In 1974, Bill Ligon sought out the help of an orthodox rabbi to learn the Old Testament principles of the spoken blessing. The previous year the Ligons had experienced a pastoral change, leaving a large church in downtown Brunswick, Georgia. They were now pastoring a new church made up of people eager to experience more of God's presence and to find solutions to problems in their lives. The Ligons had seen biblically that God's plan to favor His people was somehow embodied in the principles of blessing they were discovering in both the Old and New Testaments. It was Bill's visit with his friend, the Jewish rabbi, which opened up new areas of study and research for him.

Once Bill had researched the principles of spoken blessing, he began to teach them to the members of his congregation and to impart spoken blessings to them. The results were outstanding. Children who were failing in school began to make good grades. Businesses that were floundering began to succeed. Strained relationships between family members were often healed when family member were verbally blessed on a regular basis. Curses that had held families bound into failure began to disappear. The plan of God was working.

Bill's research revealed that God had given Moses three instruments to use when he led the children of Israel out of Egypt. The use of those three commanded practices changed an enslaved, depressed people into a strong, viable nation. The three instruments were (1) the **Blood Covenant**, which, when used on Passover night delivered the Israelites from Egyptian bondage. (2) The **Ten Commandments (Torah)** given at Mt. Sinai which gave the Israelites definition and purpose as a nation as they obeyed the commands of God and last (3) the **High Priestly Blessing** found in Numbers 6:23-27 which released the favor of God upon them. God planned for those three foundations to always be in place in the lives of His people. Just as the Israelites were made strong by them, so will people be made strong today.

Bill realized in his research that the blood covenant and the commandments (Word of God) were still in place in the church, but the High Priestly Blessing was missing. Just a few clergy in some liturgical churches were using thle blessing and then only as a ritual. Families in the churches were uninformed about God's plan for the blessing. Only Jewish Rabbis and some devout Jewish families practiced the blessing as God had commanded it. As a result, they were experiencing God's favor in a special way. While in prayer, Bill received a mandate from God to teach the principles of the verbal blessing and to challenge Christians to bring it into place as a part of the life of the churches and families. He and his wife Dorothy Jean have been challenging others with these teachings since 1974.

Now the challenge has been given to the Ligons to provide practical, hands-on training to families in small groups where serious learning is encouraged and new habits are formed. Families are encouraged to make the spoken blessing an integral part of their family life. Those who accept the challenge experience the release of God's favor and learn to share what they have learned with others.

# Beginning The Family Blessing Program

## Who Should Participate?

As many members of your household as possible should be enrolled in the Family Blessing Program. However, you should not fail to enroll if a family member is unable or fails to participate! The fact is, having an uncooperative family member is more reason to acquire as much knowledge and understanding of the Biblical plan of blessing as possible.

## Children At Meetings

All children old enough to read or understand discussions should be a part of family participation in the classes. Arrangement should he made for child care of younger children outside the class. Each family should sit together. Do not allow the children to sit in a separate group during the class but have them remain with their parents. Children should be encouraged to participate in the class discussion and should give reports on their participation in the homework assignments.

Children of Torchbearers and Journeymen families should be encouraged to participate in the class discussions and help by giving leadership in the class. Their example will be an encouragement to the children of the other families to participate constructively to the class. NOTE: Children of leadership parents should be encouraged to see themselves in leadership, and especially to encourage the children of the other families to give whole-hearted dedication to the classes.

# What The Class Is Like

During the next eight weeks, you will commit yourself to think blessing in everything you do at home, work, and school. Here is what you will be doing during the eight weeks:

1. Attend a 1 1/2 to 2 hour class each week for eight (8) weeks.

2. Prepare your homework assignments (**as a family**) for the next class by:

    A. Reviewing the last class discussion for the next class.

    B. Reading the assignment (**as a family discussion**) for the next class.

    C. Exercise practical, hands-on practice of the assignment (**blessing each other at home**).

Your class time will have the following format and you are encouraged to be faithful to stay on schedule as closely as possible.

| | |
|---|---|
| Fellowship Time (Families arrive, greet each other) | 10 minutes |
| Praise and Worship | 10 minutes |
| Discuss Last Weeks Homework & Report from Families | 20 minutes |
| Break Time (refreshments) | 15 minutes |
| Viewing the DVD Lessons | 20 to 40 minutes |
| Discussion, Question and Answer & Homework Assignment | 10 minutes |
| Dismiss with Prayer | |

# The Size Of The Class

Each class should consist of the Torchbearer Family, the Journeyman Family and five other families. No class should begin without at least the Torchbearer Family, the Journeyman Family (if possible) and two additional families. The Torchbearer Family should begin a group even if they are unable to enlist a Journeyman family to be in training. Perhaps a new family can be enlisted from the group once the class begins.

# Registration - No Fee

All individuals or families need to register for the class. The form is provided by calling us at (912) 267-9140. We will correspond with you from time to time through email. You can unsubscribe at any time. The Torchbearer family (lead family) will need the "Study Guide" and DVD's. Students will need the "Study Guide". When a Journeyman family elects to become a Torchbearer family to establish and lead a new group, they will need to purchase a set of DVD's. Additional materials listed at the back of the book. Prices may vary from the time of this printing.

# Partnering with The Father's Blessing

The Father's Blessing holds the highest respect for the local church and its pastor and is committed to strengthening the families of each local congregation. We are convinced that the stronger family relationships become the healthier the church will be. We do ask that you consider partnering with us in this ministry to take this encouraging, life giving word to others who need to know. Please partner with us by participating in a study group, leading a study group of your own, praying for this ministry and staying in contact with us. We also ask that you consider becoming a financial contributor to further the knowledge of God's spoken blessing to other families. Thank you for partnering with us.

# Practical Application

New habits are not formed easily; therefore it is important that each family member in the class participate in the exercises discussed in the material. Some may feel that they are only "acting it out" when they participate on one of the assignments. That is because they are doing something new and that leaves an uncomfortable feeling with some. However, with practice, they will become comfortable with their assignments and grow to enjoy them. Children will genuinely begin to notice a difference in their lives and begin to look forward to the exercises.

# Lesson 2

# Blessing God's People - A Biblical Overviews

"On this wise ye shall bless the children of Israel..." (Numbers 6:23)

God's first act after creating Adam and Eve was to speak blessing over them. "So God created man in His own image...And God blessed them, and God said unto them, 'Be fruitful, and multiply...'" (Genesis 1:27-28). Thus, God gave special grace to man by imparting the power of fruitfulness to him through the blessing. This action of God is only the first of many Biblical references where the practice of blessing, was observed.

## The Blessing of Fruitfulness

**Noah:**
- And God blessed Noah and his sons, and said unto them, Be fruitful, and multiply, and replenish the earth. Genesis 9:1 KJV

**Abraham:** God spoke over Abraham
- I will make my covenant between me and thee, and will multiply thee exceedingly. Genesis 17:2 KJV.
- And I will make of thee a great nation, and I will bless thee, and make thy name great; and thou shalt be a blessing: Genesis 12:2 KJV

**Melchizedek king of Salem:** Spoke a blessing over Abraham.
- Blessed be Abram of the most high God...who hath delivered thine enemies into thy hand." (Genesis 14:19-20a).

Abraham received this blessing following the victory he gained over Chedorlaomer and the kings who were with him. Hebrews 7:1 notes the importance of the act of blessing, in which Melchizedek included the giving of bread and wine to Abraham, the symbols of the body and blood

f Jesus Christ. It was significant for Abraham. Hebrews 7:7 develops
e experience further by saying, "And without all contradiction the less
 blessed of the better". Melchizedek imparted divine favor to Abraham
rough the spoken blessing. In return, Abraham gave one tenth of all he
ad earned to Melchizedek.

### Rebekah:

- received a spoken blessing from her family when she prepared to leave to be married to Isaac. They said, "Thou art our sister, be thou the mother of thousands of millions, and let thy seed possess the gate of those which hate them." (Genesis 24:60b).

### Ruth and Boaz:

- were blessed by their people just before their marriage. In Ruth 4:11, the people imparted the blessing by saying over the bride, "We are witnesses, The Lord make the woman that is come into thine house like Rachel and like Leah, which two did build the house of Israel: and do thou worthily in Ephrathah, and be famous in Bethlehem." (When Jesus was born in Bethlehem that blessing was fulfilled).

**The concept of blessing takes on greater significance in chapter 27 of Genesis.**

### Isaac:

- Isaac made preparation to speak blessing over his oldest son before he died. (27:1-4)
- The occasion was of such importance that it included a meal in which the elderly patriarch was served his favorite dish before speaking the blessing. (27:4)
- Rebekah devised a skillful plan to insure that the blessing was spoken over her younger son, Jacob. (27:5-10)
- The power of the spoken blessing was confirmed: It was said to be irrevocable once delivered (Genesis 27:33).

- The strength of blessing was confirmed: Isaac spoke a second blessing over Jacob before he left to seek a wife (Genesis 28:1-4).

When we add to those two blessings a third one spoken by th Lord Himself over Jacob during a dream, we have strong evidence support the authority of the first blessing spoken by Isaac (Genesis 28:1 -15).

**Jacob's personal desire to be blessed** demonstrates th importance he placed upon the spoken blessing. Genesis 32:24-3 graphically illustrates the value Jacob placed on the spoken blessin After wrestling with the Angel of the Lord all night, he declared, "I wi not let thee go except thou bless me."(v.26) the text goes on to say, "An he blessed him there." (v.29b). God later gave more support to the li and ministry of Jacob by speaking an additional blessing over hir (Genesis 35:9-12). The Lord imparted to him grace to be fruitfu multiply and see his children become kings to the nations. He also gav Jacob a blessing to succeed materially.

**Jacob blessed his family:**
- He impressed upon Joseph the importance of the blessing by referring to the blessing God spoke over him at Luz in the land of Canaan (Genesis 48:3).
- The 48th chapter of Genesis is a touching example of the value the Hebrew family placed upon children.
- Joseph stood his two sons, Ephraim and Manasseh before his father Jacob, who then proceeded to speak a blessing over them. Genesis 48:16
- Joseph was blessed as his father began to speak the blessing over his sons. Genesis 48:15
- When Jacob said, "In thee shall Israel bless, saying, God make thee as Ephraim and Manasseh:"(Genesis 48:20), he instituted a practice of blessing children which is still observed today in Jewish households.
- Jacob spoke blessings over all twelve of his sons before he died. Genesis 49

Jacob's blessings spoken to his twelve sons in Genesis 49 onstitutes a series of tribal blessings in which all the members of each tribe received the blessing given to their leader. A similar ritual was observed by Moses just before his death as recorded in Deuteronomy 33.

### The Priestly Blessing

God's concern for the welfare of His people is highlighted in umbers 6:22-27 when He commanded Moses to teach <u>Aaron and his ons to bless the sons of Israel.</u>

He then gave Moses a three-part blessing which He required to be poken over His people each time they assembled together. Known nong Jewish people as the "High Priestly Blessing", it was expected to woke the blessings of the Lord Himself when it was spoken.

In Leviticus 9:22 Aaron lifted his hands toward the people and lessed them. The words Aaron spoke were the same as those found in umbers 6:24-26. The positive effect of the community blessing was to e felt throughout the twelve tribes as they settled in the land of promise. was spoken over everyone of them, no one was left out.

> **The Lord bless you, and keep you;**
> **The Lord make His face shine on you;**
> **And be gracious to you;**
> **The Lord lift up His countenance on you;**
> **And give you peace**.

In like manner, blessings which parents speak over their mily should affect every area of family life.

**<u>King David</u>** said: "For the sake of my brothers and my friends, I ill now say, 'may peace be within you'. For the sake of the house of the ord our God, I will seek your good." (Psalm 122:8-9). David did seek e good of his people as demonstrated by his desire to bless them in the ame of the Lord after he had brought the ark back into Jerusalem. (II amuel 6:18).

## New Testament Blessing

The New Testament offers evidence that the practice of blessing was common among the Jewish people and was continued in the life of the church.

### Jesus Christ:

- Jesus began His three year training program with His disciples with a series of blessings.
- The beatitudes listed in Matthew 5 are a series of blessings accompanied by corresponding rewards.
- He said to His disciples, "Ye are the salt of the earth" and "Ye are the light of the world."

At that time, the disciples were neither salt nor light, yet Jesus said that they were.

- Some of them had serious character defects which would take time to correct.
- They were unregenerated men who would not know the joy of being born again until after the crucifixion and resurrection of Jesus Christ.
- Many of their old habits, such as Peter denying Jesus and cursing during Jesus trial, were still unbroken.

In spite of all that, Jesus was able to bless them by declaring them to be effective witnesses in the world. **The act of speaking that kind of success over their lives was a blessing which became a reality.**

### Jesus:

- Jesus again demonstrated His confidence in the power of the blessing when He blessed children.

Mark 10:16 states that "He took them up in His arms, put his hands upon them, and blessed them." What did Jesus say to the children when He blessed them? We can expect that He spoke encouragement to them about their futures, adding the words of Jacob in Genesis 48:20, "God make thee as Ephraim and as Manasseh." Although we do not now for a fact that He spoke those words over the children, it was the custom in His day to do so. Most certainly He spoke life and encouragement to them.

The same is true of the content of Jesus' speech when He lifted up his hands and blessed the people as He ascended into heaven (Luke 24:50). Jewish custom leads us to believe that Jesus spoke the High Priestly blessings of Numbers 6:23-66 over them.

His commitment to the principle of blessing could not be more intensely declared and less understood than in His words in Luke 6:28, "Bless them that curse you, and pray for them which despitefully use you."

### Paul:
- The same attitude is carried forward in the writing of the Apostle Paul when he says, "Bless them which persecute you: bless, and curse not." (Romans 12:14)
- He blessed the readers of Hebrews with being equipped to do God's will. (Hebrews 13: 20,21)
- He blessed the church in Thessalonica with peace at all times and in every way. (II Thessalonians 3:16)

### Peter:
- Peter gave added support to the concept of blessing when he encouraged the believers to not return evil for evil, or insult for insult. (1 Peter 3: 8-9)
- He said they were to give a blessing instead; for they were called for the very purpose that they might inherit a blessing.
- He also greeted the believers he was writing with a blessing of grace, peace, and the knowledge of God. (2 Peter 1:2)

**Notes**

## Notes

_____

_____

_____

_____

_____

_____

_____

Such evidence in both the Old and the New Testaments leaves little doubt that God has planned for the blessing to be used to impart life to those who receive it.

As one father in New England said, "My children have seen so much good coming to them since I began to speak blessing over their lives that they would not think of leaving for school without receiving blessing."

Parents who learn to impart the blessing to their children on a regular basis can hope to see very positive results in their lives.

# Quiz - Lesson 2

1. The blessing God gave for Moses and Aaron to speak over His people is called_____

2. Once delivered, the blessing is said to be _____
   (Genesis 27:33)

3. Jacob wrestled all night with a man to receive a blessing from him. Who was he?
   _____(Genesis 32:24-30)

4. What did Paul say that we should do for people who curse us?
   _____(Romans 12:14)

5. Peter said that, instead of returning evil for evil, we are to
   _____( I Peter 3:8-9)

*Answers found at end of workbook*

# Assignment – Lesson 2

1.     Speak the High Priestly Blessing (Numbers 6: 23-26) over the members of your house-
       hold each day. Lay hands on them and speak with confidence knowing that God has
       called you to speak this blessing.

(If you are single person speak the blessing over yourself and arrange to call a member of the
group to speak blessing over them and they over you each day.)

2.     Parents choose at least one positive character trait for each child and impart it to him/her
       with the spoken blessing. Do it each day this week. (For instance, for a child who has
       had difficulty concentrating in his/her schoolwork, you would say: "May the Lord bless
       you with the ability to concentrate and retain the information you study in school..")

# Lesson 3

# The Value Of Your Child

"Lo, children are an heritage of the LORD:
and the fruit of the womb is his reward."
(Psalm 127:3)

Now we focus in on the great worth of children and God's plan to release His favor on them through the spoken blessing. **No one can place a value on your children. They are priceless gifts from the Lord,** described in the Bible as "olive plants round about the table." (Psalm 128:3b). King David was shown that his covenant children would sit upon his throne forever (Psalm 132:12c). That promise of blessing from God was fulfilled in the birth of Jesus Christ and continues to be realized in the lives of many children today. Pray that God will show you His plan for your child.

Satan sees covenant children as the greatest threat to his plans. He does not want children to come under the covenant blessings of God. That can be seen in his efforts to destroy men like Moses and Jesus during their infancy. If Satan had succeeded in destroying them, he would have blocked Gods plans for man's redemption.

- Seeing God's plan for the deliverance of the children of Israel embodied in the life of the child Moses, he prompted Pharaoh to kill all the firstborn males (Exodus 1 & 2).
- Knowing that eternal redemption rested in the life of the baby Jesus, Satan prompted Herod to slay all the male children under two years of age (Matt. 2:16).

What if he had succeeded in cutting off those two children? Redemption of mankind would have been aborted.

- Failing to impart to children the blessings of God

helps to assure Satan that he can foil God's plans for them.

- The Lord has something special that He wants to accomplish through children.
- He has placed them in the care of parents to nurture and train for the fulfillment of that purpose.
- Satan knows that and he will do everything in his power to prevent parents from imparting life to their children through spoken blessing.

The imparted blessing gives great hope to parents who are concerned about the spiritual health of their children. God has given a very clear plan in the Bible for imparting blessings to children. Parents who complete this study <u>will have a command of Scriptural principles which will help them effectively impart blessings to their children.</u>

### Children are a Sign of God's Covenant

God's covenant blessings spoken over His people included the promise of offspring.

### Adam and Eve

His first act after creating Adam and Eve was to bless them and say, "Be fruitful, and multiply, and replenish the earth, and subdue it: and have dominion over the fish of the sea, and over the fowl of the air, and over every living thing that moveth upon the earth." (Genesis 1:28).

### Noah and his sons

Noah and his sons received the same blessing from God following the flood. Genesis 9:1 says, "And God blessed Noah and his sons, and said unto them, 'Be fruitful, and multiply, and replenish the earth.'". Noah and his sons could not be fruitful and multiply without having children.

Here we have the first Scriptural evidence that God's blessing was intended to:

- Bring forth new life,
- encouraging growth
- and develop rulership among His people.

23

God made it clear to them that the bringing forth of offsprin would be a part of the covenant He was establishing with them.

"And I, behold, I establish my covenant with you, and with you seed after you;" (Genesis 9:9).

### The redemptive nature of the covenant.

God's plan of perpetuating His covenant through children wa first introduced to Abraham. Abraham's faith in God's promise rested c the confidence that his own child was an integral part of God's pla Isaac was his covenant child. The Abrahamic promise included th promise of offspring and the promise of blessing for Abraham.

"And in thy seed shall all the nations of the earth be blessed;" (Genesis 22:18).

The multiplication of offspring was an important part of God covenant with both Isaac (Genesis 26:4) and Jacob (Genesis 28:14).

The promises in the Davidic covenant are similar to those Go made with Abraham. In II Samuel 7:11-12, David is promised offsprin through whom God will establish the house of David forever. **David wa conscious of the fact that it was the favor of the Lord that woul bring about the blessings upon his household.** "Therefore now let please thee to bless the house of thy servant, that it may continue for eve before thee: for thou, 0 Lord God, hast spoken it: and with thy blessin let the house of thy servant be blessed for ever." (11 Samuel 7:29).

The future of Gods people extended far beyond the life of Davi resting on the concept of covenant children coming after him.

It is through children that God plans to impart the redemptiv benefits of the covenant. The promise of children is common to all th covenants God has made with man. Each time you look at your childre remember that they are a sign that God has not nullified His promise. Th prophet Malachi taught that the sign that the covenant blessings wer being poured out upon the people of God was that:

"the heart of the fathers were turned to the children, and the heart of the children to their fathers...." (Malachi 4:6).

## Gods covenant plan for redemption has not changed.

- He will continue His work through children who have been blessed and confirmed in the faith.
- The Lord has ordained that parents will perpetuate His redemptive work by imparting blessing to their children and teaching them to do the same for their children.

Thus God has placed great value upon the life of children. They re His plan for tomorrow, that through them the life of Jesus Christ can e given to the world.

### Educating Parents and Grandparents to Bless

Satan is doing everything in his power to cut the children off from he blessings of God, just as he attempted to do so by plotting the death f Moses and Jesus Christ. His efforts are again falling short as parents arn the value of their children in the Kingdom of God and grandparents arn to bless their grandchildren. Parents educated in God's plan for nparting the blessing will learn to bless daily, expecting the favor of iod to rest upon their children.

**The patriarchs of the Old Testament went to great length to npart blessings to their children and their grandchildren**. Jewish athers have continued the tradition, speaking special blessings over their hildren weekly. Their children have enjoyed the benefits of such ommitment to God's command to bless. That is how the benefits of iod's favor are passed on from one generation to another.

Unfortunately, the Christian church has, for the most part, failed o develop a serious practice of blessing children. That should be very leasing to Satan if he can:

- distract parents from those responsibilities and

## Notes

- keep them ignorant of the power resting in the blessing,
- he can interrupt the plan of God for raising up a covenant people for Himself.

### Blessing In The New Testament

Blessing in the New Testament falls under two main categories having to do with redemption and the imparting of Divine favor.

That is the first and most vital meaning of blessing in the New Testament. Paul says in Galatians 3:13-14 that:

"Christ hath redeemed us from the curse of the law,....that the blessing of Abraham might come on the Gentiles through Jesus Christ; that we might receive the promise of the Spirit through faith."

A special blessing comes to those who receive Jesus Christ as Lord of their lives. The curse which prevented people from receiving this blessing was broken when Jesus was crucified. Now any person who calls upon the name of the Lord can be saved, receiving the blessing God promised Abraham.

The second form of blessing mentioned in the New Testament is the one which has been neglected and, sometimes, never taught in the Christian churches. It is that blessing which commands the attention of this study. In Mark 10: 16 we are told,

"And He (Jesus) took them (children) up in His arms, put His hands upon them, and blessed them."

All the synoptic gospels record this incident, catching the interest of discerning parents to the action of Jesus. Why did Jesus lay His hands on children and bless them? What did He say to them?

We can believe that He said some of the same things that Jewish fathers have said to their children for centuries when they blessed them

26

e did it because the spoken blessing imparted special favor from God
oon the children. If that is not the case, then why did Jesus perform a
tual which has no purpose?

Jesus saw merit in speaking blessing over those He loved. Luke's
ospel records an interesting event in the ministry of Jesus. In Luke
4:50-51 Luke says,

"And He led them out as far as Bethany, and He lifted up
His hands, and blessed them. And it came to pass, while
He blessed them, He was parted from them, and carried up
into heaven."

The last act of Jesus toward His disciples was to speak a blessing
ver them. As He was speaking that blessing with His hands lifted after
ne fashion of the priests, He rose into the clouds. You can almost see
im rising with His hands out stretched speaking life, peace and success
ver His people. One of the blessings He spoke over them was the High
riestly Blessing in Numbers 6:23-26.

The apostle Peter carried the principle of blessing over into his
aching. In I Peter 3:8-9 he says,

"Finally, *be ye* all of one mind, having compassion one of
another, love as brethren, *be* pitiful, *be* courteous: Not
rendering evil for evil, not rendering evil for evil, or
railing for railing: but contrariwise blessing; knowing that
ye are thereunto called, that ye should inherit a blessing."

Husbands and wives are encouraged to verbally bless each other
ach day just as they bless their children. We are called to give blessings.

# Quiz – Lesson 3

1. Which people in your family are the greatest threats to Satan's future plans?

   _____

2. What will help to assure Satan that he can abort the plan of God for your children?

   _____

3. God's first act after creating Adam and Eve was to _____ them (Genesis 1:28).

4. The benefits of God's favor are passed on from one generation to another by means of

   _____

5. What was the last act of Jesus before He ascended into heaven? _____
   _____ (Luke 24:50-51)

6. What must we do to inherit a blessing according to Peter? _____
   _____ (I Peter 3:8-9)

*Answers found at end of workbook*

# Assignment - Lesson 3

1. As a family devotion, review the way a person is born again, discussing the wonderful blessing God has given us in Jesus Christ. Read Romans 3:23, 6:23, 5:8 and 10:6-10. Read John 3:16.

2. Review the High Priestly blessing in Numbers 6:23-26. Speak that blessing over the children each day this week.

3. Husbands and wives are encouraged to speak the High Priestly blessing over each other this week.

# Lesson 4

# <u>WHY BLESS YOUR CHILDREN?</u>

And they shall put my name upon the children of Israel; and I will bless them." (Numbers 6:27)

Blessing children accomplishes much more than merely encouraging them in their daily lives.

That was seen by the parents of Stephen who was not passing in school.

- Stephen had failed the Seventh grade the previous year.
- Now he had brought home his first report card with all failing grades for his second year repeating the same grade.

The attentive parents had:
- held conferences with the school officials,
- punished Stephen
- attempted to encourage change by offering rewards.
- They were careful to see that Stephen was in Sunday School and church each week.

In spite of all their sincere efforts, nothing was working for them.

In desperation they appealed to their pastor for prayer. Perhaps God would do something to turn Stephen's life around. When the pastor offered to teach them the Biblical principles of blessing, they readily accepted.

Soon they were applying the Biblical plan of blessing to Stephen's life,
- laying hands on him daily

- speaking success into every area where he had failed.
- Stephen's attitudes began to change.

Stephen completed the Seventh grade level that year wit high scores.

- He moved on to the next level where he continued to succeed.
- He graduated with high marks.
- He, later in life, became a commercial jet pilot.

Similar cases to that of Stephen have been experienced whei parents have learned the value of blessing their children, devoting th time necessary to learn how to bless. Their diligence in impartin blessing has paid off for their children.

### God obviously had something special in mind for Hi people when He commanded Moses and Aaron to bless th children of Israel.

There is no wasted motion in the activities of God. He does n institute rites as a matter of form. There is a purpose behind ever movement and command of God. Every activity He institutes produce life at a higher level when it is observed.

Practicing the high priestly blessing in Numbers 6:22-27 was th vehicle God obviously desired to use so that He could bless His people.

- First, God expected Aaron and his sons to obey His command and speak the priestly blessing over the people.
- Then God said that, as they invoked His name, He would be present to impart blessing to them.

"And they shall put my name upon the children of Israel; and I will bless them." Numbers 6:27

Aaron and his sons were to invoke (engage, put into action, th fe that flows from the name of God) and God would be present, nparting life to those who received the spoken blessing.

- That is the way God chose to impart something of Himself to His people.

Jesus continued to use of blessing to impart life to His followers. the Apostle Peter showed that he had learned the lesson by teaching elievers that they were to do the same thing (I Peter 3:9).

Even the experience of being born again comes about through the poken blessing. The person believes the Word and speaks life over mself by confessing that Jesus is Lord. What he speaks in faith ecomes a reality in his life. He blesses himself and the blessing of God invoked in the power of the Holy Spirit to give the person new life in sus Christ.

"But what saith it? The word is nigh thee, even in thy mouth, and in thy heart: that is, the word of faith, which we preach; That if thou shalt confess with thy mouth the Lord Jesus, and shalt believe in thine heart that God hath raised Him from the dead, thou shalt be saved." (Romans 10: 8-10)

- The fact is that everything man ever receives from God he receives by the spoken word.
- Even faith comes by hearing the Word of God.

An old Jewish fable tells of a rabbi who questioned God one day out the high priestly blessing. "Why should I bless your people when ou can do it so much better?" he asked.

God replied that He commanded the rabbi to bless, but that He as present in the blessing, imparting life to His people. Parents who nderstand that God is present in the blessing when they speak it over eir children, will be more faithful to engage in the practice of speaking essing over them every day.

## Notes

The high priestly blessing in Numbers 6:23-26 was invoked at the end of worship when the community was about to be dismissed.

- The people were to carry the benefits of the blessing with them into their homes and their work.
- The effect of the blessing was to be felt in every area of their lives;
  - their character,
  - their community relationships
  - and their relationship to God.

**The building of godly character is one of the benefits which can be expected when children receive the blessing imparted to them by their parents.**

So it was with Stephen who was mentioned earlier. Stephen began to receive new motivation to apply himself to his studies. Instead of being distracted and slothful, he became alert and attentive to the important matters in his life. Stephen's character changed when his parents began to impart life to him through the blessing - and so did his grades.

God spoke of blessing to Abraham within the context of the established covenant He was making with him. The Lord's first words to Abraham in Genesis 12:1-3 relate the blessing to covenant practices.

- **God relates to mankind on the basis of covenant**.
- All of God's activity in history is expressed through covenant.
- God guaranteed His promises with Abraham through covenant.
- Thus, when the Lord says,
  "And I will make of thee a great nation, and I will bless thee, and make thy name great; and thou shalt be a blessing' (Genesis 12:2), He was relating the promised blessings to the covenant He was making with Abraham.

Jesus also related blessing to covenant when He said,

> "And I appoint unto you a kingdom, as my Father hath appointed unto me;". (Luke 22:29)

The word, "appointed", stems from the word for covenant in the reek. Therefore, Jesus is saying that just as the Father had covenanted Him a kingdom, so He was covenanting to His disciples a kingdom.

That kingdom would be one in which the blessings of Father God ould be imparted to His children. The Lord Jesus came in covenant ith the Father to pass on those blessings to His disciples in covenant ith them.

- He accomplished that fact and released blessing through His crucifixion.

Paul expands on the concept of covenant and blessing in alatians 3:13-14, when he says,

> "Christ hath redeemed us from the curse of the law, being made a curse for us: for it is written, Cursed is every one that hangeth on a tree: "That the blessing of Abraham might come on the Gentiles through Jesus Christ; that we might receive the promise of the Spirit through faith."

Parents who commit themselves to begin to bless their children an do so
- with confidence,
- knowing that they are in covenant with Father God.
- They have the power of the blood of Jesus Christ supporting them.

God has established the bringing forth of offspring as a part of very covenant He has made with man - from Adam to Abraham, Moses nd King David.

# Notes

_____

_____

_____

_____

_____

_____

_____

_____

_____

_____

_____

_____

_____

_____

_____

_____

_____

_____

_____

_____

_____

_____

_____

_____

_____

_____

As we conclude this lesson we should be reminded that:

- The recognition that children are a gift of God and a sign that God keeps covenant with every generation helps to give confidence to parents when they prepare to impart blessings to their children on a regular basis.

- God never planned for children to be deprived of the blessing which is to be imparted to them through their parents and the religious leaders of their community.

- Recognizing the blessing as God's way of bringing the covenant into active play upon the lives of their children is one of the great responsibilities of parents.

- Knowledge of the power of the blessing and God's plan for using it will encourage concerned parents to bless their children.

As parents then understand how the future of their children often hangs upon their willingness to bless, they will devote themselves to learning how to impart the blessing. "I never realized just how powerful the blessing could be," one mother said, "...until I began to speak blessing over my hyperactive child. I see changes taking place daily as I bless him with peace, self-control and unselfish love for others."

# Quiz – Lesson 4

1.  What vehicle did God give to Moses and Aaron so that divine favor could be imparted to the children of Israel?

    _____(Numbers 6:22-27)

2.  How was the name of God to be put on (invoked over) the children of Israel?

    _____

    (Numbers 6:22 and 27)

3.  Who actually did the blessing as Aaron spoke it over the people?

    _____

4.  Everything that mankind ever receives from God comes by means of

    _____

*Answers found at end of workbook*

# Assignment - Lesson 4

1.  Pick two new godly character traits for each of your children and speak them over them this week.
2.  Have your children lay hands on each of you (the parents) and speak blessing over you.

# Lesson 5

# Three Foundations of Covenant Blessing

Moses was eighty-years-old when God gave him the incredible task of delivering millions of beaten-down defeated slaves from the strongest nation on earth. After they left Egypt they had to be prepared to conquer a bountiful yet hostile land full of warring nations and angry giants. He was to do all of this by converting them into a strong, viable nation. It was truly an incredible task.

The children of Israel had their slavery mentality ingrained in their nature. They were in desperate need of help. God moved mightily on their behalf to change them into a great nation. Their transformation is our example of God's loving desire to deliver and develop us and our children through covenant blessings.

### God's instruments of deliverance

Three foundations underpin God's deliverance and blessing for Israel. The three instruments are:

1. The **Blood Covenant**, which occurred on Passover and delivered the Israelites from Egyptian bondage.
2. The **Ten Commandments (God's law)** given at Mt. Sinai that gave the Israelites definition and purpose as a nation.
3. The **High Priestly Blessing**, which released the favor of God to them.

The three work together with the High Priestly blessing (verbal blessing), usually the least known of the three, right in the center of the sovereign plan of God. The Lord expressly commands the verbal blessing and yet few in the church know how critical and potent it is in the development and welfare of God's people. God revealed that:

- when blessing is verbalized,
- He places His name on the one being blessed and
- His power is then released.

He instructed Moses in Numbers 6:27 that the verbal blessing would put His (God's) name on the Israelites, and He would then bless them.

### Israel's Bondage

The nation of Israel was born when God told Abraham He was going to bring out of his own body a great and mighty people. He said they would be enslaved in a strange land for 400 years. After that time, He would bring them out of their bondage with great possessions and establish them in their own land.

It all happened just as God said. They became slaves in Egypt. During that time, a heavy weight of oppression was placed on Israel.

- It successfully broke their will.
- They were truly a burdened people.
- Any healthy form of identity was crushed by the endless stress placed on them.
- Their hearts were defeated (low self-esteem)
- God described them as afflicted and sorrowful.

Yet, God's deliverance was at hand.

**Read Exodus 3:1-10**

**God showed His concern for Israel. The New testament is filled with evidence that God is just as concerned about you and your children.**

## The First Instrument
## The sacrifice and blood of the Passover lamb

Israel had to be released from slavery. God executed a fin
judgment that shifted the thoughts and hearts of everyone in Egypt.
brought judgment on Pharaoh and released Israel.

God required every household to:
- take an unblemished lamb and care for it in their home for tl
first 14 days of the month,
- slay that Passover lamb at twilight,
- put its blood on the doorpost of their home,
- be fully clothed and ready to leave,
- roast and eat the lamb in haste,
- eat all of it and leave none,
- stay inside their home until morning.

God sent a death angel to slay the firstborn in every househol
that did not obey. Everyone who feared God and obeyed was passed ove
and saved.

Pharaoh resisted God and his only son died in the judgment. H
ordered the Israelites released because God's mighty hand had broken h
will.

The blood of the lamb had saved Israel from judgment and ha
set them free from slavery. They followed God right out of Egy
carrying with them the people's wealth.

**Read Exodus 12:1-31**

**In like manner the blood of Jesus Christ delivers the repentant
sinner from bondage to sin.**

## The Second Instrument: "The Law"

Israel was free! Their lives were in transition and they were being defined. God had suddenly revealed Himself on their behalf. Now they needed structure so they could walk with God in a pleasing manner. It would be foolish for them to offend Him. He loved them and had delivered them.

It would also be destructive for them to devour each other in civil unrest. God gave them the Ten Commandments. He taught Israel "this is who you are and this is how you act so set your heart on it". A new path was created providing fellowship and blessing with God and in social harmony with themselves and others. It was revelation of how they could continue with God in the covenant relationship that had begun at Passover. God would be their God and perform awesome works for His treasured people. They simply needed to be His law-abiding people. They agreed.

**Read Exodus 20:1-17 and Exodus 24:1-4**

Israel entered into a perpetual covenant that promised them God's continued presence and blessings if they obeyed His commands.

This covenant:
- Was the key to their future health and prosperity.
- Determined their peace with other nations.
- Affected the land they worked and the flocks they raised.
- Showed God's blessing was now the might and measure of their increase.

God had declared they would be a great and mighty people. His glory rested on them and He was taking them to new heights. However, God's blessing was not just going to develop behind the scenes. God would get the glory. Otherwise, Israel would think it was because of their own efforts that they had been blessed. God designed a protocol to activate this covenant blessing.

**Read Deuteronomy 28:1-14**

### The Third Instrument: The High Priestly Blessing

The Lord commanded Aaron and his sons, the Priests, to speak blessings in the name of the Lord over the people. By doing so:

- God placed His name on the people and
- He then blessed them.

As God's favor was spoken over Israel, they would reach their greatest potential. Their eyes would be set on the Lord and they would rest in knowing God's blessing was theirs. It would divert idolatry and promote worship of Jehovah their provider. Their blessings came from the Lord. God commands the Priestly blessing in Numbers 6:23-26 and references it being carried out in Deuteronomy 10:8 and Joshua 8:30-33.

Two reasons why blessing works:

- God's love for us and
- the glory of His name.

God determined that His name would be glorified through the lips of His covenant people so He fused His name and their blessing together. To that end, He instructed the High Priest to bless the people and to do so in the name of the "Lord" because His name is the performance guarantee.

God does not take His own name in vain. This act of obedience by the High Priest caused God's favor to transfer and rest on the people. Their lives were overtaken by God's kind favor and His glory began to manifest on them.

**Who speaks the blessing? <u>We Do!</u>**

**In whose name? <u>The Lord's Name!</u>**

**Who does the blessing? <u>The Lord God!</u>**

## Jesus

The three foundations God used to establish the nation of Israel were shadows and examples of what God has eternally accomplished for us in Jesus.

- Jesus defeated the power of sin and curses (the Pharaohs we face) and
- Was the fulfillment of the law (Matt. 5:17)
- gave gifts to men (the blessings we receive).
- He is the complete eternal embodiment of the three foundations mentioned.

The picture of our need for Jesus becomes evident when we look into God's law. So we will begin by looking into the law first.
**Read John 8:34-36**

## Our Pharaoh and Bondage

The Ten Commandments show us our Pharaoh. They awaken us to our bondage to **sin and the curse of sin**. It becomes evident when we compare our life to the commandments that we sin. It is in our nature to do so. We are rebellious and unrighteous. Actions produced out of our corrupt nature always cross the line of God's Commands. Romans 3:23 says "For all have sinned and fall short of the glory of God."

God prophesied in Isaiah 61 and Jeremiah 31:31-34 complete freedom from sin and bondage. He declared the exchange of our unrighteousness for the righteousness of Christ. He did so in the new covenant He made with Jesus. The oath was that

- God would anoint and send His Son Jesus into the world to do His will.
- Then He would apply the benefits of this finished work to those who repent (turn to God) and believe.
- Then we receive Jesus, His resurrected life, and the Holy Spirit.

Jesus faithfully obeyed. He kept the Law (the old covenant) and

## Notes

_____

_____

_____

_____

_____

_____

_____

_____

_____

_____

_____

_____

_____

_____

_____

_____

_____

_____

_____

_____

_____

_____

_____

accomplished His Father's will (the new covenant). Hebrews 10:5-10 te
us that Jesus paid our debt and set us free that we might live in faith ar
obedience to Him. The three instruments God gave to Moses are no
found in the ministry of Jesus.

### The First Instrument: Jesus our Passover Lamb

**Read John 1:29a, 34 and Hebrews 9:11-15**

Jesus was the Passover Lamb and the eternal High Prie
administering the new covenant. He was sacrificed at the time c
Passover. (Exodus 30:10 & Luke 22:15,16) He took our sins in His bod
and in His death judged our sin. The blood He shed was the etern
atonement for all sin. Then He arose to administer the victory He wo
The curse and bondage of sin was broken. Our sin was judged just a
Pharaoh's bondage was judged. The blood of Jesus freed us from th
power and slavery of sin and curses! When the covenant blood of Jesus
in our hearts, the death angel of eternal damnation passes over us.

### The Second Instrument:
### The Law of the Spirit, alive in Christ Jesus

**Read Romans 8:2 and Galatians 5:16**

Jesus finished His work on earth and returned to His Father. H
sent us the Holy Spirit to
- empower us to apply the promises of the new covenant to ou
  lives and
- teach us all things.
- lead the born again believer out of sin and on to maturity.
- tell us about things to come.
- empower us to do the good works God prepared for us.
- grow in the grace and knowledge of God.

As a result, we have a new law based on the completed work c
Christ and the presence of the Holy Spirit. The law is that if we walk i
God's Spirit we will not fulfill the lust of the flesh. Sin has no mor

ominion over us. The commandments (law) are fulfilled in the redemptive ministry of Jesus. (Mathew 5:17)

### The Third Instrument: Bless and Curse not

**Read 1 Peter 2:9, Luke 24:50-51, Ephesians 1:2, 1 Peter 3:9-12, and Mark 10:13-16**

The third instrument, the verbal blessing, is magnified in Christ. We have become a royal priesthood and a holy nation. Jesus has become the High Priest of our confession. The priestly authority and responsibility to speak blessing has spilled over to everyone who is born again.

Peter and Paul continuously verbalized blessings in their letters to believers. They did so invoking God's name as they blessed. They expected the transfer of God's favor to be on those they addressed. Jesus laid His hands on children and spoke blessing over them. He blessed His disciples. The last act He performed was to speak blessings over the gathered people who saw His ascension.

The protocol given in Numbers 6:23-26 to activate God's covenant blessings is observed fully by Christ and the New Testament writers. They too fused together God's name and spoken blessings. It is an instrument of spiritual transfer. The command to bless has expanded to all believers due to the great liberty and grace found in Christ Jesus.

# Quiz– Lesson 5

1.    What were the three foundational instruments that God used to set Israel free from the bondage of Egypt and transformed them into a victorious, viable nation?

_____

_____

2.    Who commanded that the blessing be spoken_____

3.    Choose the letter below that correctly begins the priestly blessing.
A. I bless you …
B. May the Lord bless you …

4.    When the verbal blessing is spoken, who is doing the blessing?_____

5.    The blessing must be spoken in faith? True or False          (Hebrews 11:21)

*Answers found at end of workbook*

# Assignment - Lesson 5

1.    Each day this week read the Ten Commandments together as a family  and talk about each one.

2.    Lay hands on each other each day and bless each other
   • Parents bless the children.
   • Husbands blessing their wives.
   • Wives blessing their husbands.
   • Children blessing their parents.

Note: The book "The Bee and The Bear" and the CD with the ten children's stories on the Ten Commandments will help children appreciate the value of them in their lives.

# Lesson 6

# THE REDEMPTIVE POWER OF THE BLESSING

"And he blessed them that day, saying, In thee shall Israel bless, saying, God make thee as Ephraim and as Manasseh: and he set Ephraim before Manasseh." (Genesis 48:20)

When we look at the Scriptures to understand the power of the blessing, evidence surfaces to show that God's plan for blessing is a redemptive one.

## It is made on the principle of divine substitution.

The older son lays down his rights to the birthright in favor of his younger brother. The entire experience is expressed in prophetic terms as it points to the time when Jesus Christ comes in response to man's cry for a blessing from God.

- God hears the cry of the sinner for mercy and
- blesses him by imparting the blessing of His first-born, Jesus Christ, to the sinner.
- The effect of the blessing of salvation is that God substitutes the life of Jesus for the life of the sinner.
- The sinner, who deserves to die, lives instead.
- The Savior, who deserves to live, dies in his place.

When the thought of seeking a blessing for Ephraim and Manasseh was first introduced in Genesis 48:1,
- the first-born, Manasseh, was named first.
But when the elderly Jacob spoke of his grandsons,
- he reversed the order and named the younger Ephraim first (v.5).

## Notes

Joseph then proceeded to place his small sons before his father so that his right hand would fall on the head of Manasseh, the older one, and his left hand would fall on Ephraim's head (v.13). Joseph's plan of having Manasseh receive the blessing of the first-born failed when

- Jacob extended his hands to speak blessing over the two boys
-  crossing his arms so that his right hand fell on the head of the younger Ephraim and
- his left hand fell on the head of the older Manasseh (v.14).

### The Right Hand of Blessing

The right hand was considered the hand that imparted the greater blessing. (Jesus Christ is seated at the right hand of the Father in heaven.

Therefore, it displeased Joseph to see his father imparting the greater blessing to his younger son, Ephraim (v.17). He then attempted to move his father's right hand from the head of Ephraim to Manasseh (v. 18).

- Jacob refused to reverse the position of his hands, saying that he knew what he was doing (V.19).
- Then he proceeded to pronounce a blessing in which he put Ephraim first.

The order in which Jacob blessed his Grandsons was of such vital importance to the act of blessing that the text calls attention to it: "and he set Ephraim before Manasseh." (v.20b).

Joseph knew the custom of granting the greater blessing to the first-born who, in turn, was expected to become responsible for the tribe when the father died. It was a double-portion blessing in which the older received twice as much inheritance as the younger. The extra inheritance was needed to oversee the responsibilities of the tribe when the father died.

It came as a total surprise to Joseph that his father reversed the order of blessing, imparting the greater blessing to the younger.

46

Jacob blessed Joseph by blessing his sons, causing the firstborn blessing to fall upon him also. Speaking to Joseph, Jacob says,

"Moreover I have given to thee one portion above thy brethren..." (v.22).

Ruben was actually the first-born of Jacob. His blessing over Ruben formally removed the first-born blessing from him: "Unstable as water, thou shalt not excel", Jacob declared as he blessed Ruben (Gen. 49:4a). Later when Jacob spoke his last blessing over Joseph, he finalized the transfer of the first-born blessing from Ruben to Joseph:

"The blessings of thy father have prevailed above the blessings of my progenitors unto the utmost bound of the everlasting hills: they shall be on the head of Joseph, and on the crown of the head of him that was separate from his brethren." (Gen. 49:26)

### Jacob gets Esau's Blessing

Further evidence of the effect of divine substitution upon the blessing is found in the birth of Esau and Jacob. While the twins struggled in Rebekah's womb, the Lord said to her:

"the elder shall serve the younger." (Gen. 25:23b)

The prophecy was fulfilled in the plan of Rebekah who hastily prepared Isaac's favorite dish, disguised her younger son, Jacob, and sent him before his blind father to receive the first-born blessing.

The strength of the blessing with its legal application is found in a part of the blessing which Isaac spoke over Jacob:

"be lord over thy brethren, and let thy mother's sons bow down to thee:" (Gen. 27:29b).

Even after the plan was uncovered, Isaac allowed the blessing to stand (v.33), upholding the fact that the younger had received the blessing which belonged to the firstborn.)

## Prophecy Revealed

There are two other passages of Scripture which shed light on the meaning of the blessing imparted to Jacob. They are found in Malachi 1:1-3 and Romans 9:1-16. The people complained in Malachi 1 that God did not love them.

"I have loved you, saith the LORD. Yet ye say, Wherein hast thou loved us? Was not Esau Jacob's brother? saith the LORD: yet I loved Jacob, And I hated Esau.. ."(Mal. l:2-3a).

Understanding of God's answer through Malachi is given by Paul in Romans 9. Paul talks about the deep longing in his heart to see Israel saved. He stated that he would be willing to be separated from Christ for the sake of his brothers (v.3). He then recalled the prophecy God gave to Rebekah in Genesis 25 when He said,
"The elder shall serve the younger."(v.12).

And finally, he referred to Malachi's words when he said,

"As it is written, Jacob have I loved, but Esau have I hated."(v.13).

This Scripture relates salvation to the blessing, given to Jacob. By using Jacob's experience of receiving the blessing, of the first-born:

- Paul has identified the relationship between the preferred place in Isaac's blessing, and
- the preferred status when the sinner receives the life of Jesus Christ in place of punishment for his sins.
- The sinner reaches the place that he realizes his lost condition places him in a hopeless state.
- He appeals to God for deliverance, crying, 'Lord, be

merciful to me a sinner."

- **God, in response, reaches into the life of His first-born, Jesus, and takes the blessing from Him to give to the repentant sinner.**
- The new life the sinner receives is the life of Jesus.
- Jesus, in return, gets Calvary.

### Divine Preference Shown

God shows divine preference when He gives eternal life to a sinner. The sinner deserves to die because of his sins. Jesus, who was without sin, deserves to live. But God sends Jesus to the cross to die in the sinner's place and transfers the life of Jesus over to the sinner. **The sinner receives the resurrection life of the firstborn as a blessing.**

Considered in that light, the words of Paul in Galatians 3:13-14 are replete with revelation:

"Christ bath redeemed us from the curse of the law, being made a curse for us: for it is written, Cursed is everyone that hangeth on a tree: That the blessing of Abraham might come on the Gentiles through Jesus Christ; that we might receive the promise of the Spirit through faith."

The act of willfully giving up His birthright is reflected in the words of Jesus in Matthew 20:28 when He said:

"…the Son of man came not to be ministered unto, but to minister, and to give his life a ransom for many."

Paul says in Philippians 2:8 that Jesus:

"humbled Himself, and became obedient unto death, even the death of the cross."

## Notes

One difference between Jesus and Esau is that Jesus willful released His birthright that it might be given to sinners. Esau resented th substitution and allowed bitterness into his spirit instead of honoring th redemptive plan of God.

### Jews Bless Like Father Jacob

The blessing Jacob spoke over Ephraim and Manasseh has bee repeated many times through the ages by dedicated Jewish fathers as the imparted blessing to their children. A part of the blessing includes th words, "May God make you like Ephraim and Manasseh."

Using this rite on the Sabbath to impart blessing to their son Jewish fathers have repeatedly acknowledged the redemptive plan of Go who would impart blessing to all mankind through the Messiah who wa to come.

Christian literature seems to be almost entirely void of an reference to seeing the blessing as a redemptive rite which acknowledge God's plan of salvation being imparted to man. The opportunity missed to take the principles of blessing and use them for the childre Therefore, a rich heritage has been lost to the church and to children wh need the opportunity to receive blessings.

Malachi said that the people questioned whether God loved them The prophecy shows that:

- they were people bound to their circumstances.
- They judged God's love by the way God blessed the materially.

**But God placed the appraisal of His love on the basis of divin preference.**

"Was not Esau Jacob's brother? saith the LORD: yet I loved Jacob…" (Mal. 1:2-3a).

That same divine preference occurs with sinners. Believers often ...dge Gods love for them by the way He blesses them materially.

"But God commendeth His love toward us, in that, while we were yet sinners, Christ died for us." (Romans 5:8).

Paul says it is clear that God still shows His love through divine ...reference. Jesus crucified at Calvary is the evidence that God loves the ...l people.

Each time Jewish fathers have spoken the blessing of Ephraim ...nd Manasseh over their sons, they have declared that preference without ...alizing its full significance.

When parents speak blessings over their children today, they too ...eclare the preference of God for their children. Every child has the right ...have that preference spoken over his life many times.

**Many children who are in trouble will be released from ...ondages when they receive blessings.**

Girls in Jewish households receive another blessing which ...eserves out attention. Each Sabbath, the daughter stands before her ...arents as the father says, "May the Lord make you like Rachel and ...eah, both of whom built the house of Israel."

Rachel and Leah brought forth from their households all of the ...eads of the twelve tribes of Israel. Their sons became heads of state. ...hey were leaders of nations. The words of the blessing come from the ...ook of Ruth in chapter 4:11-12 where a blessing was spoken over Boaz ...nd Ruth by the townspeople. They said:

"The LORD make the woman that is come into thine house like Rachel and like Leah, which two did build the house of Israel; and do thou worthily in Ephrathah, and be famous in Bethlehem."

That blessing came true to the fullest as Boaz and Ruth became the grandparents of King David and the ancestors of Jesus who was born in Bethlehem. The townspeople did not know how Boaz and Ruth would become famous in Bethlehem. They spoke the blessing. God did the rest.

When parents begin to understand the redemptive power of the blessing, they will take the time to impart blessings to their children on a regular basis.

# Quiz – Lesson 6

1.  Joseph placed his oldest son, Manasseh, so that the _____ hand of his father Jacob would fall on his head (Genesis 48:13).

2.  When Jacob crossed his arms, his right hand fell on the head of the younger _____ (Genesis 48:14).

3.  The hand considered to be the one imparting the greater blessing was the _____ hand.

4.  Blessing the younger over the older was a shadow or type of the Christian's relationship to God's first-born son: _____

5.  Through the blessing of Abraham, the sinner receives _____ and Jesus receives? _____

6.  When Jewish girls are blessed, their parents say, May the Lord make you like _____ and _____ who built the house of God.

*Answers found at end of workbook*

# Assignment - Lesson 6

1.  Have a discussion with the children about the transfer of the first born blessing from Jesus to them resulting in receiving the gift of eternal life (the life of Jesus in them).

2.  Identify the dreams and ambitions of each family member and speak blessings over each one, trusting God to release His favor over them to achieve those goals. (For instance, to a child you could say: "May the Lord bless you with the ability to excel in your class as an excellent student.")

# Lesson 7

## Jacob Found His Blessing

**Notes**

God reveals in Genesis 18:19 that He chose Abraham for the purpose of directing his children and his household after him to keep the way of the Lord by doing what was right and just. That way God would bring about for Abraham the promises He spoke over him. It was important that Abraham taught his children what he learned from the Lord. The welfare of the next generation was on the line. Abraham's attitude was that of wholehearted obedience when God told him to sacrifice his beloved son Isaac in the region of Moriah. He immediately made preparations and left. (Genesis 22)

Abraham's attitude towards obedience, according to Genesis 18:19, makes a point. The lives of his children were a witness to the world of the lessons God taught Abraham because he was faithful to walk it out and pass it on. From that small deduction we know for sure that the Lord taught Abraham the power of imparting blessing. We can see that Isaac walked in God's blessings and blessed his sons just as Jacob did with his sons and grandsons. Had Abraham's children not learned this from their father, they would not have practiced it in such great faith with their own children. (Gen 25:11, 26:12, 48 and 49)

We can look to Abraham's grandson as the example because much is said about him in Genesis. Jacob's life demonstrates the divine fulfillment of spoken blessings. This Lesson will briefly outline Jacob's discovery of blessing, his desire to gain it, his development by receiving it, and his determination to walk out a life of faith and obedience to God. Also in the sections labeled "blessings fulfilled" we can see the power and demonstration of God's blessings being applied to Jacob.

## Jacob's Discovery (Gen 25:27)

Jacob's understanding of the Lord's blessing was learned from the stories his father and grandfather told as he grew up. He was convinced about God's covenant faithfulness. He determined to receive his verbal blessing.

- Genesis tells that Jacob grew up staying around the tents. He spent a lot of time around Abraham and Isaac where as Esau spent much of his time out hunting game.
- Jacob was described as a quiet man and that would make him more prone to listening.
- Abraham lived with him among the tents and impacted his life for 15 years before he died at age 175.
- Jacob lived 40 years with his father Isaac before he received the firstborn blessing.

### Jacob heard

- Jacob heard about God's power, protection, and grace when He delivered Abraham from the power of kings and pharaohs. Gen 12:17 Gen 20:3
- How God had called Abraham to slay Isaac
- Abraham's obedience and Isaac's rescue. Gen 22
- He heard the stories of God cutting covenant with his grandfather Abraham. Gen 12, 15 and 17
- He learned the purpose and power of the spoken blessing God had spoken over Abraham. Gen 12, 15 and 17
- He learned the blessings that Abraham had spoken over his father Isaac.
- The Lord appeared to Jacob and confirmed the covenant relationship that existed with his father Isaac and grandfather Abraham along with their obedience to Him. This confirmed to Jacob God's approval of his parents and grandparents lives and the lessons that

they shared with him.

### Jacob saw

- God multiply his father's crops a hundred fold in the midst of a famine. Gen 26: 1&12
- God protect his parents' lives and marriage from king Abimelech. Gen 26:8
- His father meet with the Lord and the Lord renew His covenant with Isaac. Gen 26:2-6

Certainly his heart was stirred by these stories to the point of desiring a personal covenant relationship with God where His favor and blessing became his very own.

### Jacob's Desire

Jacob's desire for God's blessing was fueled by what he learned at home. He was moved to the point of taking personal risks to see that he was in the middle of grace. He believed in its value and he would not be left out. Gen 25:29-34, 27, 32:24-26

- He was not the firstborn yet he boldly offered to trade the birthright inheritance of Esau's for a bowl of stew.

- To gain the blessing he risked losing his life from his angry brother.

- At the risk of receiving a curse from his blind father he obeyed his mother's command (Gen 29:5-13) masqueraded to gain the firstborn blessing spoken over him thus fulfilling God's promise to release the firstborn blessing to the younger.

- The Angel of the Lord appeared to Jacob on his journey back home from Laban's home. Jacob grabbed Him and wrestled with Him all night saying he would not let Him go until he received a blessing.

**Jacob's Development** (The blessing he received)

27 "And he came near, and kissed him: and he smelled the smell of his raiment, and blessed him, and said, See, the smell of my son is as the smell of a field which the LORD hath blessed: 28 Therefore God give thee of the dew of heaven, and the fatness of the earth, and plenty of corn and wine: 29 Let people serve thee, and nations bow down to thee: be lord over thy brethren, and let thy mother's sons bow down to thee: cursed be every one that curseth thee, and blessed be he that blesseth thee." Gen 27:27-37 KJV

**Isaac spoke this blessing in the name of the Lord over Jacob.**

- **The dew of heaven** – spiritual blessings of life, strength, and refreshment from God's throne, extending God's authority and life to be rained down on Jacob. Spiritual blessing meant spiritual fruit and character: love, joy, peace, patience, kindness, goodness, faithfulness, gentleness, and self-control.

- **The fatness of the earth** – to bless the health and wealth of his soul and body. All the natural provision he could need would be given in abundance. This more than met the needs of being sustained. He was given abundance described as more than needed (fatness).

- **And plenty of corn and wine**: It goes along with the fatness of the earth so that what he had been given would be sustained and sustained with joy.

- **Let people serve thee and nations bow down to**

_____

_____

_____

_____

_____

_____

_____

_____

_____

_____

_____

_____

_____

_____

_____

_____

_____

_____

_____

_____

_____

_____

_____

thee: He was given favor in relationships with neighbors, business acquaintances, and those who were in authority. It promoted peace and respect.

- **Be lord over thy brethren and let thy mother's sons bow down to thee:** He was receiving the firstborn blessing to accommodate the responsibility of maintaining the household. He would need order and unity for the household to survive and prosper because a divided house would not stand.

- **Cursed be everyone that curseth thee and blessed be everyone that blesseth thee:** An atmosphere of protection and favor was conveyed. The people Jacob would relate to would become aware that they were blessed if they blessed Jacob and they were cursed if they cursed him. That was a make-or-break proposition that wise men would soon figure out.

Jacob received one more blessing from his father Isaac. Rebekah his mother, was looking out for Jacob's safety because of Esau's anger and threat. She asked that Jacob travel to her brother's home and marry from their own people and not from the daughters of Canaan. Isaac spoke this blessing saying,

"And Isaac called Jacob, and blessed him, and charged him, and said to him, Thou shalt not take a wife of the daughters of Canaan. 2 Arise, go to Padan-aram, to the house of Bethuel thy mother's father; and take thee a wife from thence of the daughters of Laban thy mother's brother. 3 And God Almighty bless thee, and make thee fruitful, and multiply thee, that thou mayest be a multitude of people; 4 And give thee the blessing of Abraham, to thee, and to thy seed with thee; that thou mayest inherit the land wherein thou art a stranger, which God gave unto Abraham." Gen 28:1-4 KJV

**Jacob's Determination** (The fulfillment of Blessing)

Jacob, in Genesis 27, finally received the blessing he longed for. ver his lifetime he faced many hardships that were life-threatening, stressful, or just plain aggravating, yet God's hand was with him. He ew in the blessing. His new lease on life was bound to the blessing and t in the hardships he faced.

Jacob left home immediately following the blessing. Strangely ough he left to go on a 400-mile journey back to Haran with nothing ore than the staff in his hand. It seems he would have been given plenty f provisions but he wasn't. What he did have proved life-giving to him. e had the blessing Isaac spoke over him in faith and his staff, the sign f authority that was placed in his hand. Gen 32:10 The first night of his urney the Lord appeared to him in a dream. What happened next is ally extraordinary to ponder.

10 And Jacob went out from Beer-sheba, and went toward Haran. 11 And he lighted upon a certain place, and tarried there all night, because the sun was set; and he took of the stones of that place, and put them for his pillows, and lay down in that place to sleep. 12 And he dreamed, and behold a ladder set up on the earth, and the top of it reached to heaven: and behold the angels of God ascending and descending on it. 13 And, behold, the LORD stood above it, and said, I am the LORD God of Abraham thy father, and the God of Isaac: the land whereon thou liest, to thee will I give it, and to thy seed; 14 And thy seed shall be as the dust of the earth, and thou shalt spread abroad to the west, and to the east, and to the north, and to the south: and in thee and in thy seed shall all the families of the earth be blessed.  15 And, behold, I am with thee, and will keep thee in all places whither thou goest, and will bring thee again into this land; for I will not leave thee, until I have done that which I have spoken

—————————————
—————————————
—————————————
—————————————
—————————————
—————————————
—————————————
—————————————
—————————————
—————————————
—————————————
—————————————
—————————————
—————————————
—————————————
—————————————
—————————————
—————————————
—————————————
—————————————
—————————————
—————————————

to thee of. Gen 28:6-15 KJV

God opened Jacob's eyes so he could see what he had strived so hard to gain. God showed him what he had received from his father. The dream was a vision of God's blessing in a nutshell. The Lord's angel would deliver the blessings, minister to Jacob, and report back. The provision and way of life was real. Jacob had believed it but now he could see it. It was the same provision that Jesus spoke to Nathanael about when he said:

> Verily, verily, I say unto you, Hereafter ye shall see heaven open, and the angels of God ascending and descending upon the Son of man. John 1:51 KJV

- Vs. 12, the gate and path was open
- Vs. 12, the angels were ascending and descending ready to
    - Bring the dew of heaven (spiritual gifts and refreshing)
    - The fatness of the earth
    - An abundance of corn and wine
- The Lord stood at the top of the ladder showing that He was going to do the blessing.
- Vs. 13, God affirmed to Jacob that He was the God of his father. God was true to the words that Jacob's father and grandfather obediently spoke over him.
- Vs. 14, Jacob was going to receive the wife and family that he was going to his uncles to find.
- Vs. 15, Jacob was shown that God's safety and presence went with him wherever he went and he was given the assurance that God would accomplish all that was spoken over him.

Then Jacob made a vow that if the Lord would keep him safe on the journey and give him food to eat and clothes to wear that the Lord would be his God. He also vowed to honor Him by tithing 10 percent of what God gave him. Gen 28:20-22

Jacob arrived safe at his uncle's home and stayed for the next 20 years. He helped Laban by shepherding his flocks. A month later Laban asked him what his wages should be. Jacob said he would work seven years for his youngest daughter Rachel. The years seemed like nothing to him and when they were complete he was ready to marry. He was given Leah instead since she was the oldest. A week later he was given Rachel and she also became his wife. He agreed to work another seven years for her. Gen 29:14-30

During the second seven years Jacob worked for Laban, Jacob fathered eleven boys and one girl. Gen 29:32-30:22 God blessed him with quite a large family in a short period of time. Likewise, Laban's flocks prospered under Jacob's management. Gen 30:27 At the end of his fourteen year obligation Jacob wanted to return to his father's house to begin building an inheritance for his own family. Laban, however, was eager to keep Jacob around because the little he had when Jacob arrive had greatly multiplied.

### Blessings fulfilled

- Jacob arrived at his uncle's home safe.
- Jacob was married to Rachel and Leah and in seven years fathered eleven boys and one girl fulfilling the blessing the Lord and his father spoke over him for marriage and children.
- Jacob agreed to marriage in exchange for his labor. Laban blessed Jacob by giving him a home, food, safety, and his daughters as the agreed wage. Laban's flocks grew and he became prosperous. (God blessed Laban because he blessed Jacob.) Gen 30:27

Laban asked Jacob to stay and once again negotiate his wages. Jacob offered a plan that God had shown him in a dream. Laban accepted. Gen 31:10-12 The Lord also reminded Jacob of the previous dream he had of the ladder and the Lord at the top of the ladder. He also reminded Jacob of his vows. It may have seemed to Jacob like the

blessing was delaying but the Lord was reminding him that it was nc
God was still in charge and He was about to abundantly deliver Isaac
first blessing. Gen 31:13 Gen 31:43

Later, God tells Jacob that it is time to go back to his father'
house. During the six-year period Jacob worked for Laban, Laba
cheated him. Yet Jacob's wealth grew and Laban's dwindled. Gen 31:4
Because Laban's attitude towards Jacob had changed for the worst, Jacc
fled for home when Laban was away shearing his sheep. This wa
discovered and Laban gathered a band of men to confront Jacob. H
intended to do Jacob harm and take away his family and all h
possessions. God intervened with a strong rebuke to Laban and peac
was made between the men. Jacob lost nothing. Gen 31:19-52

### Blessings fulfilled

- Before Laban asked Jacob to stay and work longer, the
  Lord appeared to Jacob and reminded him of the
  dream he had fourteen years before. {1)The ladder
  with the angels ascending and descending and the
  Lord standing at the top, and 2)the vow he had made.}
  God was showing Jacob his blessing of "the fatness of
  the earth" was coming.
- God blessed Jacob by giving him a divine plan to
  increase the herds that belonged to him. Jacob obeyed,
  starting with few, and at the end of six years was
  incredibly wealthy.
- Laban changed the wages that Jacob was to receive ten
  times, but no matter how he arranged it Jacob's flocks
  grew and his dwindled
- Because the new bargain for wages was violated by
  Laban's cheating, Laban was losing his flocks. God
  cursed him for cursing Jacob.

Jacob became afraid of Laban and foolishly left without sayin
goodbye. Laban in his anger caught up with Jacob intending to do hir
harm. God in a dream intervened for Jacob. In a warning the Lor

buked Laban telling him not to harm Jacob. God kept Jacob safe.

Jacob was then brought word that his brother Esau was on his way to meet him with a large band of armed men. Jacob was afraid and evised a plan to pacify his brother who had wanted to kill over the essing. He split his possessions into two bands and sent ahead valuable fts of various livestock, donkeys, camels, sheep and the like to offer as fts in order to pacify his brother. He stayed back while this was appening and prayed to the Lord, crying out for his own safety. After e prayer he made his own preparations to survive the peril he now ced. He was alone and the Angel of the Lord appeared to him. Jacob abbed Him and did not let go of Him demanding, "I will not let thee , except thou bless me".

26 And he said, Let me go, for the day breaketh. And he said, I will not let thee go, except thou bless me. 27 And he said unto him, What is thy name? And he said, Jacob. 28 And he said, Thy name shall be called no more Jacob, but Israel: for as a prince hast thou power with God and with men, and hast prevailed. 29 And Jacob asked him, and said, Tell me, I pray thee, thy name. And he said, Wherefore is it that thou dost ask after my name? And he blessed him there. 30 And Jacob called the name of the place Peniel: for I have seen God face to face, and my life is preserved. Gen 32:26-30 KJV

Jacob, now Israel, met his brother Esau and found grace. They owed affection for each other and were reconciled. Gen 33:4 Jacob oved back to his homeland, built an altar to worship the Lord, and ttled in with all the abundant provisions with which the Lord has essed him. He settles in Shechem. Gen 33:18-20 There he and his mily went through many trials that ended with Jacob feeling threatened y his neighbors. The Lord told him to go back to Bethel. He returned fely and the Lord appeared to him again to pronounce a blessing over im.

9 And God appeared unto Jacob again, when he came out of Padan-aram, and blessed him. 10 And God

said unto him, Thy name is Jacob: thy name shall not be called any more Jacob, but Israel shall be thy name: and he called his name Israel. 11 And God said unto him, I am God Almighty: be fruitful and multiply; a nation and a company of nations shall be of thee, and kings shall come out of thy loins; 12 And the land which I gave Abraham and Isaac, to thee I will give it, and to thy seed after thee will I give the land. 13 And God went up from him in the place where he talked with him. Gen 35:9-13 KJV

Jacob set up an altar and worshiped the Lord who had appeared to him. As they moved on to Ephrath, Rachel gave birth to his twelfth son Benjamin and died from a difficult labor. The nation of Israel was born in the conception of his twelve sons.

When we see Jacob again he is well along in years and he is again restored to Joseph, who he thought was dead. Joseph fulfilled God's plan for his life and saved his family, Egypt, and the surrounding nations from the effects of a seven-year famine that devastated the world. The family was brought to Egypt and given the best land to live in and pasture their animals. Gen 47:27 The final passages written of Jacob before the Lord took him on home to heaven speak of the blessings he bestowed on his grandsons Ephraim and Manasseh. Gen 48 He also spoke blessing over all his sons that were appropriate to them in Genesis 49. After speaking those blessings, he drew his feet up into his bed, breathed his last breath and died.

Jacob lived an amazing life filled with hope, difficulties, blessings, and restored joy. He kept the vow he made to the Lord. He was a servant of the Lord who worshiped, walked, and talked with Him. There was no other for Jacob. God kept him and fulfilled the blessings He and Isaac spoke over his life. The blessings Jacob received were fulfilled in the midst of the ordinary and extraordinary moments of his life.

### Blessings fulfilled

- When Jacob and his family traveled, God put a fear of them in the hearts of the surrounding people so they would not attack this wealthy family to harm or rob them Gen 35:5
- Jacob was kept safe during the famine and lost none of his family or property
- Jacobs's son was used to bless the people of the world at the time by administering a food program for pharaoh during a famine. All the nations of the earth were blessed by him, fulfilling a spoken blessing.
- Jacob blessed Joseph's two grandsons.
- Jacob's last act testified one more time to the authentic place and work of the verbal blessing in the kingdom of God. It is recorded as the last thing he did before he pulled his feet up in the bed and God took him on home.

# Quiz - Lesson 7

1. Jacob learned to bless his children from his father_____ and his grandfather _____.

2. The blessings Isaac and God spoke over Jacob resulted in many good benefits for Jacob.
   A. True   B. False

*Answers found at end of workbook*

# Assignment - Lesson 7

1. Have each family member name at least one benefit coming to him/her as a result of the blessings spoken over his/her life.

2. Every day this week lay hands on each family member and speak blessings, including the High Priestly Blessing in Numbers 6:23-26.

# Lesson 8

# Learning From The Patriarchs

"By faith Isaac blessed Jacob and Esau concerning things to come. By faith Jacob when he was a dying, blessed both the sons of Joseph; and worshiped, leaning upon the top of his staff." (Hebrews 11:20-21)

Isaac and Jacob's practice of imparting blessing to their children was of such importance that it found its place in the hallmark of faith in Hebrews, chapter 11. The Holy Spirit attests to the importance of blessing by acknowledging its place within the family of believers. Informing themselves about the use of blessing by the fathers of the Bible will help parents bring rich rewards into the lives of their children and each other. Parents are blessed with the satisfaction of seeing their children enjoy the benefits that come from the blessing. Husbands and wives will begin to enjoy the benefits of God's grace released through blessing.

It should be said that imparting blessings is not a sure guarantee that children will respond positively or that there will not be any failures.

- Jesus took twelve men and imparted blessings to them, accompanied by teaching from the scriptures. Although they studied three years with Jesus, He was successful with only eleven of them. The twelfth one betrayed Him.
- King David was a man who knew how to bless, yet one of his sons, Absalom, stood at the gate of the city and turned the people against his father.

However, it can be said that the success rate of the fathers of the Bible was much higher than the families in the churches today. For the most part, the church has failed to teach the people to bless one another. Where families have recovered the lost art of imparting the blessing, the ave seen remarkable results in the lives of all the family members.

"My seven year old daughter was a bed-wetter", one father
lates. "We tried everything from punishment to rewards. She did not
spond to us or to medical help. Then the Word of God began to heal
er. My wife and I heard about the power of the blessing. After studying,
e principles, we began to:

- speak life over our daughter.
- We blessed her with self-control and confidence.
- We blessed her with a new self-esteem and
- assurance that she was loved and appreciated by the family.

Her bed wetting soon stopped and her self-respect increased
reatly. She never wet the bed again."

Everyone enjoys hearing the story of a person who was healed by
e Word of God. But it is evident that even the Bible does not promise
ne hundred percent success with the blessing. On the other hand, that
ould not discourage parents from imparting blessings to their children.
ailures among children are reduced to a minimum when parents are
ithful to bless them with the Word of God.

Greater success is realized when children are taught to desire the
essing like Jacob.

### Isaac's Training

Isaac is known as the child of promise. He was aware that
mething special was about to happen when Abraham went to offer him
s a sacrifice before God (Genesis 22). Isaac was certainly old enough to
nderstand what was happening because his father laid the wood for the
crifice on his shoulders for the last part of their journey together (v.6).
e heard the Angel of the Lord remind Abraham that God's blessings
pon his seed (children) were a part of His covenant plan for Abraham.
e witnessed the faithfulness of God in providing a ram as a substitute
r his own life.

# <u>Notes</u>

The knowledge that Isaac gained from those experiences and the lessons he received from his father prepared him to bless his own children when he was old.

## Making Preparation To Bless

• Isaac took the initiative himself to prepare for a special blessing to be spoken over his son Esau.

• He understood that the blessing had deep significance in the life of his son. Therefore he said, "Prepare a savory dish for me such as I love, and bring it to me that I may eat, so that my soul may bless you before I die."

• Isaac wanted to be in the right frame of mind when he spoke the blessing because his words would significantly affect the future of his son.

• He was about to speak forth a blessing, which, in his society, would serve as a last will and testament.

The preparation taken in these lessons to prepare for the blessing is of vital importance in preparing parents to give the blessing and children to receive it.

**Isaac's entire life was filled with blessing rites which**

- **formed character in him and**
- **provided direction for his life.**

That is not so for the average church member today. <u>The absence of family traditions which provide insight into the purpose of the blessing requires that parents who wish to bless take time to study and understand the principles of blessing given in the Word of God.</u>

Those parents who gain the conviction that the blessing will enrich the lives of their children will consistently use the blessing to strengthen their lives. The same is true with husbands and wives who arn to bless each other on a daily basis.

In Genesis 28:1 Isaac blessed Jacob the second time, including in the blessing a charge that he would not marry an unbeliever. Marriage is a covenant which greatly influences the faith of the marriage partners. The patriarchs took care to insure that their children married within the limits of the covenant established with Jehovah God. When Esau wanted to rebel against his parents out of spite, he married unbelievers. (Genesis 8:8). Parents should be careful to begin early to bless their children with godly wives and husbands. The way they word their blessing will greatly affect the decisions the children make later when they choose their life partners. Such blessings from the parents should come out of the deep convictions of their own hearts. If they do not believe what they are saying, they will not have much power when they impart the blessing.

### Avoiding Isaac's Folly

There is a flaw in Isaac's understands of blessing which deserves attention. Isaac suffered conflict in his spirit when he prepared to bless his sons because he ignored an important word from the Lord. In Genesis 5:21-23, the Lord spoke in prophecy to his wife, Rebekah, telling her that she was going to have twins and that the older **would** serve the younger. When Isaac prepared to speak the blessing of the first-born over his son Esau, he should have remembered the Word of the Lord. His partiality for his first-born, Esau, caused him to overlook the prophecy and prepare to speak the first-born blessing over Esau. Only through the action of Rebekah was Isaac able to avoid being disobedient to the Lord's command.

Giving more attention to the will of the Lord could have helped Isaac prepare his sons for the pronouncement of the last will and testament which was given in the form of a blessing. He could have spoken the first-born blessing over Jacob and another blessing over Esau without provoking Esau to wrath.

Parents who plan to use the blessing should prepare early,

planning something special for each child in their family. Care should b taken to avoid partiality in anything that is said during the blessing.

## Letting Grandparents Bless

Jacob's experience in his old age brings to light the place grandparents in imparting the blessing. Looking again at Genesis 4 Jacob, who was very weak, gathered his strength and sat up in his be when Joseph entered with the two grandsons. Jacobs attention to then claiming them as his own, serves as a source of encouragement grandparents to consider the responsibility of imparting blessing to a their grandchildren. The place of grandparents in the lives of childre cannot be overstated.

One family prepared all the grandchildren for a special vis before the grandparents. The grandchildren were lined up beginning wit the oldest. The grandparents were seated side-by-side in two chairs t allow them to extend their hands to bless the children. When the young children saw their older cousins kneel before their grandparents and bo their heads to receive a blessing, they followed in line and did the same.

Before the blessings were finalized with the youngest, th presence of the Lord was manifested in the room, moving the childrer parents and grandparents into a time of special reverence before the Lor Grandparents have the capacity to bless with great anointing.

## The High Priestly Blessing

The high priestly blessing given in Numbers 6:23-26 highligh the importance of the entire family or community of believer participating in times of blessing. Aaron and his sons were taught to ble the sons of Israel by saying to them, "The Lord bless thee, and kee thee".

- The blessing was stated with "The Lord bless you" not "I bless you".

- The wording of the blessing is an acknowledgment that it comes from God.
- The purpose is to bless the people with protection from the evil of the world.
- The blessing of care and protection should be spoken over the children and the family **daily.**

The second part of the blessing says, "The LORD make his face shine upon thee, and be gracious unto thee;". The face of God is the personality of God expressed in loving favor to man. Sometimes, God turns His face away in disfavor and chastisement. David prayed, "Make Thy face to shine upon Thy servant:"(Psalm 31:16a). The face of the Lord shining upon children results in special blessings being bestowed in their lives. Imparting that blessing could only result in good for your children.

The final part of the blessing states, "The LORD lift up His countenance upon thee, and give thee peace." (Numbers 6:26).

- That speaks of a manifestation of power upon the people,
- resulting in peace on their lives.
- It is the total of all the good which the Lord does for His people.
- This blessing will release special favor upon the children, making it easier for them to experience success in their lives.

All three parts of the priestly blessing should be spoken over children at some time during a blessing service. Peter says that we are a chosen generation, a royal priesthood..." (I Peter 2:9a). Learning to impart the blessing to children and others for whom we are responsible is an excellent way to begin to function as priests. When it is done in faith, should release many blessings upon those who receive the blessing.

# Review – Lesson 8

1. God's plan for Esau and Jacob was that the _____ should serve the
_____ (Genesis 25:21-23)

2. Who saved Isaac from imparting the first-born blessing to the older son Esau?
_____ (Genesis 27)

3. What Old Testament passage emphasizes the importance of grandparents blessing their
grandchildren? _____

4. What passage of Scripture highlights the importance of families participating in times of
blessing together? _____

*Answers found at end of workbook*

# Assignment - Lesson 8

1. Parents are asked to write out the good character traits they want in their children. Make
a separate list for each child.

2. Each day this week, bless each child with the character traits on your list.

# Lesson 9

# How To Bless Your Children

"And all the people departed every man to his house: and David returned to bless his house." (I Chronicles 16:43)

We have seen in this study the principles upon which the blessing established in the Word of God. Parents should be encouraged by the fact that the Lord is the one who blesses when they invoke His name over their children. Children who receive blessings from their parents on a regular basis will notice the difference in their lives. It will not be long until they will ask to be blessed if the parents overlook the responsibility.

There is an old Jewish custom which helps train children to show respect and reverence for the Word of God. Jewish parents will take a dip of honey and place it on the lips of their small children. As their babies savor the sweet taste of the honey, the parents tell them that the Word of God (Torah) is as sweet as honey and much to be desired. Children, who develop a love for the Word and then receive that Word spoken over them in the form of blessing, enjoy spiritual benefits which do not come to everyone. Jewish parents who observe that custom instill in their children a deep love and respect for the Torah which makes it easy for them to receive their blessings.

### Visualizing Your Childs Success

When Pastor Ligon was a boy, He had a friend who never received blessings from his parents. They were concerned parents who took Robert to church every Sunday to help him learn to live the good life. They were critical of every mistake he made and warned him that if he did not change his ways he would turn out to be a failure in life. Robert became nearly everything his parents warned him he might become.

- They could never seem to see beyond Robert's

immediate attitude or behavior.

- Their attitude toward him was controlled by Robert's actions, not their faith.

.

Jesus related to people on the basis of the potential He saw in their lives. He saw what they would become through the Word He spoke to them daily.

He called His unregenerated, untrained disciples:
- the "salt of the earth" and
- the "light of the world" (Matthew 5-13-14).

When Jesus told Peter that he would deny Him three times, He prefaced it with the words, "when thou art converted, strengthen the brethren." (Luke 22:32b).

- He could have said, "if you are converted…", but He said "when".
- He could have told His disciples that if they stayed with Him long enough and tried hard enough they might become the salt of the earth and the light of the world.
- But Jesus was able to see the possibilities in His disciples.
- Therefore, He called them "salt" and "light".
- They were already that in the heart of Jesus, so they became what He spoke over them.

Isaac and Jacob related to their sons the same way as Jesus when they blessed them:

"By faith Isaac blessed Jacob and Esau concerning things to come. By faith Jacob, when he was a dying, blessed both the sons of Joseph…" (Hebrews 11:20-21).

It was by faith that the patriarchs spoke blessings over their children. They blessed from the heart, expecting all that they said over

74

eir children to come to pass.

Parents should pray, asking God to give them the ability to isualize the successful future of their children. With a clear vision of the otential in each child, the blessing can be spoken with authority and onfidence.

### Discipline in the Context of Blessing

Since all discipline should be designed to produce good character in hildren, correction can be given within the context of blessing.

As the discerning father turned his son over his knees to paddle im, he was heard to say, "You are a fine boy and this type of behavior has o place in your life." That father had the ability to see beyond a temporary ailure in his son's character. The son was fortunate to have a father who new how to bless even when he was disciplining him.

If the parents do not believe in the future of their children, the hildren's lives will be one up-hill battle after another.

### Desiring the Best

Isaac asked Esau to hunt game and prepare his favorite dish so that e could eat it before speaking the blessing. **Having the right attitude is mportant to imparting the blessing to your children**. Just as discipline annot be conducted out of a heart full of anger, **blessing cannot come out f a critical attitude.** David said, "Because of the house of the LORD our od I will seek thy good." (Psalm 122:9).

- Parents should work through their own feelings before they attempt to bless.
- Once they reach the point that they "seek the good" for their children, they can begin to bless.
- That attitude can sometimes be achieved through prayer, or
- the study of the Holy Scriptures.

Working through this study guide will encourage parents to prepare their souls well before they attempt to bless.

### Verbalizing the Blessing

Every blessing in the Bible is a verbal one.

Genesis 1:28 says, "And God blessed them (Adam and Eve), and Go said unto them…"

David said, "For the sake of my brothers and my friends, I will now sa May peace be within you."

- The blessing is always a spoken one,
- **not just a desire hidden in the heart of a parent**.
- Words have power when they are released.

Loving parents should find it easy to choose effective words t impart blessings to their children. Those who are accustomed to bein very quiet may need to give special attention to developing the art c communication through the spoken word. God instructed Moses to spea to Aaron and his sons about imparting blessing to the sons of Israel. H said, "Thus you shall bless the sons of Israel, You shall say to them: Some parents who normally are non-verbal about their faith wi demonstrate great ability to express themselves when called upon to bles their children after deciding to speak up and bless.

When Pastor Ligon picked up the telephone, the excited voice o the other end of the line said with joy, "Pastor, I must tell you wha happened to me today. I was sitting listening to your tapes on Impartin the Blessing, when I suddenly felt remorse that my father could not bles me. I had never heard him pray, read the Bible or express a desire t attend church. Almost at the same moment on the tape, you said tha some would think that their parents could not bless them for a lack c spiritual commitment in the parent's life. You went on to say that Go would honor their office and that the blessing imparted from them woul have a positive effect on the child who received it. I went hom immediately and asked my father to bless me. After I explained to hir what the blessing was all about, he laid hands on me and spoke the mos wonderful blessing I could imagine. Pastor, I feel that I am floating abou vo feet off the ground."

Her father who was normally silent about his faith, had
rought the words forth out of a heart full of love for his daughter. We
ever know what will come out of our mouths when we choose to speak
fe over our children.

## Laying on of Hands

Joseph drew his two young sons very close to his father,
cob, so that he could lay his hands on the boys. Mark 10:16 says that
sus "took them (children) up in his arms, put his hands upon them, and
lessed them." The church has been faithful to practice the laying on of
ands for the ordination of church leaders. In some cases, churches have
reserved the work of healing through the laying on of hands. Yet few
ave taught the parents of the church to lay hands on their children and
less them. The rite is observed in many Jewish homes each Sabbath.

Children should be taught to kneel before their parents in
xpectation as they lay their hands upon their heads and impart blessing
them. As the hands come to rest upon the children, they will learn to
xpect God to impart special favor to them.

## The Blessing Irrevocable

Paul said in Romans 11:29 that "the gifts and calling of God are
ithout repentance." That is, they are irrevocable. The permanency of the
lessing spoken in faith gives strength to the children when they receive
.

Isaac confirmed that the blessing, once given, had permanent
alue in the life of the one who received it. When Esau returned from
unting game and preparing his father's favorite dish, he and his father
saac learned that someone else had already received the firstborn
lessing. Upon hearing it, the text says that "Isaac trembled very
xceedingly". After inquiring as to whom it was that he had already
lessed, Isaac said almost abruptly, "yes, and he shall be blessed...

(Genesis 27:3).

Blessings have great authority in the lives of the children wh
will receive them. And no one can take their blessings away if the
respect them enough to keep them.

# Quiz – Lesson 9

1. Jewish parents place a dip of honey on the lips of their small children and tell them the Word of God is as _____ as honey.

2. Parents must _____ success in their children in order to bless them.

3. Jesus related to people on the basis of the _____ He saw in their lives.

4. The Patriarchs blessed their children by _____ (Hebrews 11:20-21)

5. Parents can bless their children and _____ them at the same time.

6. Every blessing in the Bible is a _____ one.

*Answers found at end of workbook*

# Assignment - Lesson 9

1. Parents and children should continue to bless each other everyday this week.

# Lesson 10

## How To Break The Curse

"Bless them which persecute you: bless, and curse not." (Romans 12:14)

Suzette was a nice looking lady, 35 years of age, who had grown larger by the day until her physician told her she was dangerously over weight. He suggested a stomach by-pass to correct the problem, explaining that the procedure posed certain dangers which were probably outweighed by that of continuing to carry the excess weight.

Suzette had failed in every weight-loss plan she had tried. Her lonely evenings were spent in her apartment regretting the last piece of pie she had eaten and condemning herself as she stood before the mirror. Her frustration was aggravated more by the constant failure to succeed at any effort to maintain a diet plan. Any weight loss, which would be minimal, would be followed by weight gain. She just did not know what to do until her doctor suggested corrective surgery to control her food intake for her.

Pastor Ligon first learned about Suzette when her mother called. "Suzette has a problem with her weight that is serious, Pastor. The doctor has recommended surgery. Would you talk to her?" He was confident that Suzette could get help from God if she made an honest effort to understand the biblical principles of blessing. When Suzette came to see him, he found that she was eager to find a solution to her problem and he was anxious to teach her the Bible way of breaking the curse.

- "You are speaking curses on yourself", he told her.
- "You look in the mirror and tell yourself you are ugly and fat."
- "You do not see the girl you can be in Christ Jesus your Lord."
- "Why don't you try it God's way and see what He will do for you?"

Suzette was a diligent learner, taking scriptures to heart and speaking them over herself every day.

- "I apply Bible verses to myself every day just like I would take a prescribed medication", she said.
- She selected the weight she wanted to set as a goal for herself and
- blessed her self with that weight.
- When she looked at herself in the mirror, she told herself she was a lovely girl and that in the heart of God she was not fat.

Weeks later, Pastor Ligon felt a tug on his coat as he stood at the entrance to the church building. He turned to see Suzette with her hand behind her head turning in circles like a fashion model. "How do you like the way I look, Pastor?" she asked. In the next breath she exclaimed,

**"I have lost seventy-two pounds!"**

"He could hardly believe my eyes. It was more than he had expected. "We spent a long time rejoicing over the power of God which had worked for Suzette", he said, "it was a good example of how the power of the blessing works over the curse."

**The Curse of The Law**

Two different types of curses are named in the New Testament, both of which greatly influence our lives. The Apostle Paul talks about the first curse in Galatians 3:10:

"For as many as are of the works of the law are under the curse: for it is written, Cursed is every one that continueth not in all things which are written in the book of the law to do them."

That curse upon mankind was broken in the crucifixion of Jesus Christ.

"Christ hath redeemed us from the curse of the law, being made a curse for us: for it is written, Cursed is every one that hangeth on a tree:" (Galatians 3:13).

Our Lord took the full impact of punishment for sin in His own body at Calvary, releasing us from the consequences of sin. "For the wages of sin is death…" Paul emphasizes in Romans 6:23a.

All informed believers rejoice in the fact that the blessing of Abraham has broken the curse of death over them. It happens each time a sinner turns to God from his sins and receives Jesus Christ into his life as Lord and Savior. At that moment:

- God supernaturally breaks the curse over the sinner,
- God delivers him from the power of darkness.
- It is a marvelous act of God's grace granting to every repentant believer new life and freedom from the curse.

Paul describes that condition as a blessing. In Romans 4:6-8, he says:

> "Even as David also describeth the blessedness of the man, unto whom God imputeth righteousness without works, saying, blessed are they whose iniquities are forgiven, and whose sins are covered. Blessed is the man to whom the Lord will not impute sin."

That is the message of the New Testament. Redemption from the curse of the law is present in the blood of Jesus Christ. That blessing has been well proclaimed by the church.

### The Malediction

A malediction can best be described as a curse. The power of the curse is stated both in the Old and New Testaments. Genesis 12:3 quotes God as saying:

_____
_____
_____
_____
_____
_____
_____
_____
_____
_____
_____
_____
_____
_____
_____
_____
_____
_____
_____
_____
_____
_____
_____

"And I will bless them that bless thee, and curse him that curseth thee..."

The bitterness of the curse is described in James 3:10-11:

"Out of the same mouth proceedeth blessing and cursing. My brethren, these things ought not so to be. Doth a fountain send forth at the same place sweet water and bitter?"

For the most part, the church has neglected the teachings in the New Testament on the way to break the power of the curse. Pa highlights the power of the blessing over the curse when he says:

"Bless them which persecute you: bless, and curse not." (Romans 12:14).

Stephen, the boy mentioned in lesson 3 of this study, learned t power of the blessing over the curse. His parents began to speak blessi over his life so they could break the curse of failure over him. B something else happened which was a great source of encouragement Stephen.

**He was taught how to break a curse over his own life.**

Stephen had misbehaved so often in the classroom that t teachers had him marked as a trouble-maker. "No matter what you ( now to reform, some teachers will look on you as a failure", Past Ligon told him. "You must learn the power of the words of Jesus Luke 6:28a which say,

**"Bless them that curse you".**

Pastor Ligon said, "I had Stephen approach my desk sever times as if I was the teacher and he wanted my blessing instead condemnation. He finally learned his part well. Then I prepared him return to school the next day and bless his teachers who were no cursing him. Arriving at each classroom throughout the day, I pproached the teacher and said, "I am very sorry for the way I have cted in your class and I ask you to forgive me. I do want to change and ecome a good student. You are a fine teacher. If you will help me I now I can learn in your class."

Pastor Ligon had warned Stephen that at least one teacher would ot believe anything he said. He was prepared for her. He stood erect and stened quietly as she dressed him down. "Who are you trying to fool", he snapped back. "You are just a troublemaker. You have caused me ore trouble than anyone in all my classes. You will never make nything out of yourself. You are a failure now and you will always be ne."

When she had finished, Stephen replied, "I understand how you el and I am sorry that I have caused it. But you are an excellent teacher. /ith your help, things will be different." the teacher's attitude changed nmediately and life turned around for Stephen as he broke the curse ith the blessing.

From then on, he enjoyed the daily blessings of his parents over is life. His grades all changed from failure to high scores. Stephen was n his way to success, and to become a jet pilot.

**Inheriting A Blessing**

Peter said in I Peter 3:9b:

"but contrariwise blessing; knowing that ye are thereunto called, that ye should inherit a blessing."

Inheriting a blessing is predicated in this passage upon:

- **the willingness of the believer to give a blessing to someone else.**

Peter had already taught in chapter 2 that the behavior of Jesus nder suffering was an example of the way His followers should react to persecution.

"For even hereunto were ye called: because Christ also suffered for us, leaving, us an example, that ye should follow his steps."

Peter goes on to point out that:
- no bitterness was found in Him.
- He chose not to revile back when He was reviled or
- to threaten when He suffered.

On the contrary:
- He is found praying for his tormenters when He suffers on the cross (Luke 23:34).
- Jesus was faithful to His own words in Luke 6:28 when He said, Bless them that curse you, and pray for them which despitefully use you."
- Every believer should follow his example as God's way for breaking the curse.

### The Power of Good Over Evil

The Apostle Paul said that we were not to be "overcome of evil but overcome evil with good." The words of Peter in I Peter 3:13 agree:
"And who is he that will harm you, if ye be followers of that which is good?"

The fact that good is greater than evil is established. S Augustine compared good and evil to light and darkness. Darkness only the absence of light. So evil is the absence of good just as darkness is the absence of light. No one ever turned on the darkness. If we were a brightly lighted room, we would not attempt to turn down the light turning up the darkness. But we can dispel the darkness by turning up the light. In like manner, we can bring on the darkness by removing the light Blessing is one way of turning on that light.

**When we allow unjust criticism, anger and bitterness to com from our mouths, we are attempting to overcome darkness wit**

arkness.

We never overcome evil with evil - only with good. As Hannah :ayed and ministered to the Lord following the birth of Samuel, she :clared:

> "Talk no more so exceeding proudly; let not arrogance come out of your mouth: for the Lord is a God of knowledge, and by Him actions are weighed." (I Samuel 2:3).

What comes out of our mouths makes a difference in the way we :e able to overcome evil directed against us. Our actions are weighed.

**When we see unacceptable behavior in our children, we can ive correction to their lives without condemning them with our ords.** A parent can place little Johnny across the knee and spank him hile speaking blessing over him at the same time.

- "You are a fine boy and what you have done is not acceptable.
- That is why you are receiving this spanking.
- You are going to grow up to be a fine man.
- I love you and desire the best for your life."

ll of that can go on while the parent is correcting the child.

There is a difference between punishment and discipline.

- Punishment is given to inflict pain for a wrong done.
- Discipline is given to develop character in the child.
- The parent who blesses while correcting the child is administering discipline.
- The parent who only punishes the child for his bad behavior, speaking condemnation over him, leaves the child under the curse of his words.

"If you don't change your ways, you will probably end up just like your uncle, in jail for ten years", the insensitive parent declares. An[d] more than likely, that is what will happen if the parent does not learn ho[w] to break the curse with the blessing.

### Blessing - A Sign of Maturity

Jesus instructed His disciples saying:

"Love your enemies, bless them that curse you, do good to them that hate you, and pray for them which despitefully use you, and persecute you; That ye may be the children of your father which is in heaven: for He maketh the sun to rise on the evil and on the good, and sendeth rain on the just and on the unjust." (Matthew 5:44 -45).

The command to love your enemy and bless those who curse yo[u] would be difficult to accept if one did not understand the meaning [of] verse 45.

"That ye may be the children of your father..."

The word, 'children', in this passage is actually a word whic[h] describes a mature son - a partner with his father. A better translatio[n] would be "sons".

An immature, childish Christian would have difficulty wit[h] jealousy and envy if the sun and rain soaked the crops of his neighb[or] who was an unbeliever. He would complain to God that He was not fa[ir] with him. "After all, I serve you and you bless that unbeliever just a[s] much as you do me", he would protest.

But the mature Christian:
- does not judge God's love by the way He treats other people.
- He sees himself as a partner with God.
- He sees himself having access to all the blessings of

his Heavenly Father.

- His point of reference is always the Lord, not others.
- His desire is like that of his Heavenly Father - the redemption of his neighbor, and his enemy.

As a result, he is called a "mature son" of his Father in heaven. hat makes him "perfect" or "mature" just as his Father is perfect. It is om that viewpoint that the Christian is able to bless those who curse m. Paul emphasizes that point in I Corinthians 4:12b when he says, "being reviled, we bless; being persecuted, we suffer it."

# Quiz – Lesson 10

1. The two types of curses named in the New Testament are the curse of the_____ and the _____

2. A malediction can be described as a _____

3. James 3:10-11 says that _____ water and _____ water should not come from the same fountain.

4. When Jesus was reviled and abused, He refused to _____ his tormentors.

5. St. Augustine said that just as darkness was the absence of light so _____ is the absence of _____

6. The difference between punishment and discipline is that punishment only inflicts _____ while discipline forms _____

*Answers found at end of workbook*

# Assignment - Lesson 10

1.  Have each family member list the names of people they feel have spoken curses over them. Forgive them and make plans to begin to bless them.

2.  Have each family member ask the other family members for any verbal curses they have spoken over them. Then ask forgiveness.

3.  Have each family members lay hands over the other and speak blessing over them.

# Lesson 11

# Planning A Special Blessing Service

"And it came to pass, that when Isaac was old, and his eyes were dim, so that he could not see, he called Esau his eldest son, and said unto him, My son: and he said unto him, Behold, *here am* I. And he said, Behold now, I am old, I know not the day of my death: Now therefore take, I pray thee, thy weapons, thy quiver and thy bow, and go out to the field, and take me *some* venison; And make me savory meat, such as I love, and bring *it* to me, that I may eat; that my soul may bless thee before I die." (Genesis 27:1-4)

The air was filled with expectation as the four carefully selected couples arrived at the Ligon home for the blessing service of their son. All of them had spent time in prayer to prepare for the occasion. They had chosen verses of Scripture for him which they felt the Lord had shown them related to the boy's future life. Some had written out special blessings.

Dorothy Jean had spent all day preparing one of the most exquisite meals of her life. She had bathed every dish with prayer asking that their guests would bring special blessings for their son.

She and Pastor Ligon had prayed and prepared personal blessings gleaned from a study of the Bible. The desire of their hearts was to see their son experience the favor of God. The scene was set for one of the sweetest experiences their household has ever received.

Planning a special blessing service for your child will provide an unforgettable experience for every member of your family. This study will help you plan a unique, personal blessing service for each child.

## Notes

_____

_____

_____

_____

_____

_____

_____

_____

_____

_____

_____

_____

_____

_____

_____

_____

_____

_____

_____

_____

_____

_____

_____

_____

The child who has been prepared ahead of time to expect to receive something special from the Lord will remember the experience for years to come. But the most important outcome of the experience will be the positive results for the child. Many children have recognized the lasting effects of the blessing on their lives. They learn to expect their parents to bless them regularly.

Resources For Blessing

There are seven resources to draw from to prepare you to do the best job of blessing. Creative parents will be able to develop their own ideas, using these resources as springboards to make their own plans.

**Just make sure that everything you do is in agreement with the Holy Scriptures and you will have a blessed experience with your children.**

As one happy father wrote, "I guess it goes without saying, the message the Lord gave you (about blessing) has had a tremendous impact on our family and friends." God's plan of blessing is a great source of encouragement to anyone who prayerfully uses it for the good of his family. Let us look at some of the resources which will help prepare you to bless your children.

### 1. The Desire of Your Heart

It was by faith that Isaac blessed Jacob and Esau and it was by faith that Jacob blessed both the sons of Joseph (Hebrews 11:20-21). They were able to see the favor of God resting upon their sons.

**Out of that ability to visualize the desires of their hearts for their sons, they declared their blessings.**

Jesus exercised that same grace when He was blessing His disciples. Matthew 5:3-12, commonly called the Beatitudes, is a series of blessings which Jesus spoke over His disciples at the beginning of the training period.

90

Every major experience they had is embodied in the beatitudes. They received what Jesus imparted to them through the blessings spoken in the beatitudes.

Jesus also expressed the desire of His heart when He called them the

- "salt of the earth" (Matthew 5:13) and
- "the light of the world" (Matthew 5:14).

Similar desires can be identified by parents who can then speak them over their children in the form of blessings.

- Jesus was able to see what His disciples would become through the Word He was planting in their hearts.
- He knew the Holy Spirit would take that Word and bring it to maturity in the lives of His followers.

Since the first teachings of Jesus were filled with blessings, we can believe that the disciples were encouraged to believe that everything Jesus said would take place in their lives.

In Luke 22:31-32, Jesus said to Peter,
"Simon, Simon, behold, Satan hath desired to have you, that he may sift you as wheat: But I have prayed for thee, that thy faith fail not: and when thou art converted, strengthen thy brethren."

- Jesus saw beyond the temptation and subsequent failure of Peter in his denial of Jesus to the future success of Peter.
- He said to him, "when thou art converted".
- He said "when". In spite of the fact that Jesus knew that Peter would deny Him three times (V.34),
- Jesus saw beyond Peter's unacceptable behavior to visualize his success.

Jesus could have also told His disciples that, if they stayed with Him long enough, some day they would become the salt of the earth and the light of the world. Pastor Ligon said, "That is what I would probably have done if I had attempted to train twelve unruly, unregenerated me[n] like the disciples." I would have said, "I am not sure that you will ev[er] become apostles, so you are going to have to work very hard to change.["]

**But, Jesus instilled in them the belief of what they would become even while He was teaching them the basics of their Christian life.**

Isaac and Jacob:

- used the same desire of their hearts to speak blessings ov[er] their children.
- They spoke it by faith.
- What their sons were to become was already a reality in th[e] hearts of their fathers.
- They used their desire as a resource to bless.
- With a clear vision of the potential resting in the life of th[e] child, the blessing can be spoken with authority an[d] confidence.

The blessing can also be given even during a time of discipline.

- All discipline should be given to form good character in th[e] child, not
- just to punish him for a wrong committed.

The discerning father can turn his young son over his knee an[d] say, as he is spanking, "you are a fine boy and that type of behavior [is] unacceptable. You are going to grow up to be an outstanding man."

- First, the father speaks a blessing; then he paddles him.
- That father has the ability to see beyond a temporary failure i[n] his son's character.
- The son is fortunate to have a father who can bless even whe[n] he is disciplining his son.

If parents do not believe in the future of their children, they wi[ll] hinder their progress instead of helping. Pray that God will give you [a] vision of what your child is in the heart of God - then declare that ov[er] his life!

92

Isaac understood the importance of desire. In Genesis 27:3-4, he said,

> "Now therefore take, I pray thee, thy weapons, thy quiver and thy bow, and go out to the field, and take me some venison; And make me savory meat, such as I love, and bring it to me, that I may eat; that my soul may bless thee before I die."

He wanted to feel good before he began to speak blessing over his son. Knowing that the words which would come out of his mouth would have great power in the life of his son, he planned to eat his favorite meal prepared by his son before he began to speak. Then, with appreciation, his words would flow with greater anointing over the life of his boy.

Isaac reached that attitude through eating his favorite meal. It can also be reached through prayer, fasting and a study of the Word of God. The point is that the blessing should be spoken when the desire is the greatest.

Working through this study will help to prepare your soul before you attempt to bless. Others who want to learn how to bless their children should complete this study and commit to a regular program of blessing. Then you will have a more thorough knowledge of the principles of blessings and the reasons for blessing.

## 2. Personal Insights into Your Child's Life

Your child has natural talents and abilities which have been invested in him or her by the Lord. They were born with those abilities.

The words that you speak over your children to bless the latent talents in their lives will help to bring those abilities to the surface. Many children grow up with undeveloped talents locked up inside them because the parents did not speak blessings over them as a way of encouraging the development of the talents. The patriarchs looked carefully at their children and used the talents in them to help prepare the blessing to be spoken.

### 3. Special Inspiration from The Holy Spirit

The Holy Spirit gives revelation to parents when they pray and fast about the blessings to be spoken over their children. The prophetic word comes forth many times when parents sincerely seek revelation from God before speaking blessings over their children.

The friends you invite to your home for a special blessing service should be encouraged to pray for wisdom and revelation about your child before they arrive. Many times they will bring words written out or beautifully printed to present to your child. The Holy Spirit will give special insight into the abilities of the child, providing the correct words to encourage the proper development of those talents.

The child may not be aware at the time of the blessing of the significance of all that is said. Yet, the blessings will have their positive effect on his life, Later in life he will look back upon the experience to confirm that what was said was indeed from the Lord. The words spoken will have become a reality in his life.

### 4. The Promises of God

You are encouraged to search the Scriptures to find the promises which speak to the life of your child. Then incorporate those Scriptures into blessings which you will speak over him on a regular basis. God will bless and enhance your words as you weave their names into the promises you speak.

Pastor Ligon said he had found that he could take his child's name and place it within the Scriptures in the following way, using, for instance,

Psalm 1: "Blessed is (William) that walketh not in the counsel of the ungodly, nor standeth in the way of sinners, nor sitteth in the seat of the scornful. But (William's) delight is in the law of the Lord; and in His law doth he meditate day and night. And (William) shall be like a tree planted by the rivers of water, that bringeth forth his fruit in his season; (William's) leaf also shall not wither; and whatsoever (William) doeth shall prosper."

In this way, the Word of God will come alive to you personally causing you to feel that it is directed to your child with more purpose than you would otherwise feel.

Peter, the recipient of so many personal blessings from the Lord, certainly understood the power of promises when he said,

"Whereby are given unto us exceeding great and precious promises; that by these ye might be partakers of the divine nature, having escaped the corruption that is in the world through lust." (2 Peter 1:4).

The promises of God should be collected and prepared in a special way for the benefit of your children.

**Abraham "staggered not at the promise of God" (Romans 4:20a).**

Use the promises with great confidence when you are preparing blessings for your children.

### 5. What Other People Say About Your Child

Pastor Ligon said, "When our children were growing up, people would sometimes comment on their good behavior when we were not with them. Knowing some of the attitudes Mother and I had to deal with in the home, I often wondered if they were talking about the same child I knew. Yet, after thinking it through, I realized that those friends were seeing the better part of our children. They had the ability to behave properly and they had done so at the right time. Now it could have been that those people had also seen some attitudes in our children which were less desirable - yet they had chosen not to tell us about those moments. I learned a lesson as I listened to my friends.":

- that the good in my child is more important then the bad.
- "Listening to them helped me to identify positive traits in the lives of my children."
- "Now I could concentrate on those when I prepared a blessing service."

Do not discount the possibility of using evaluative testing to help you identify aptitudes and abilities in your child. Ask for testing results from your child's school which will help you understand your child better.

### 6. The Desires of Your Child

Listening to your child will help you begin to understand the desires of his heart.

**You need to know how the desires got into his heart in the first place and whether they are noble in character.**

The child who has been allowed to view the wrong television programs or read unhealthy material will have corrupted desires. Adjustments to your child's lifestyle will result in adjustments to the desires of his heart.

One youth minister said, "When I take a group of young people away on a retreat, removing, them from television and other adverse influences, the desires of their hearts change quickly. Formerly, they desired the things of the world; now they desire the things of God."

Jesus saw desire as important to getting one's prayers answered. In Mark 11:24, He said,

"Therefore I say unto you, What things soever ye desire, when ye pray, believe that ye receive them, and ye shall have them."

It takes time to listen to your children and identify the desires of their hearts. But it is necessary if you are going to use their desires to elp you impart blessings to them.

Pastor Ligon said, "On one occasion, one of my children told me bout the desire he had for something in his life. I immediately said no ecause I did not have the personal resources to provide what he wanted. ater that day, the Lord spoke to me and said," "It does not pay to be a ood boy, does it?" "I was corrected in my spirit with the realization that had turned him down only because I could not provide it myself. I went uickly to his room upon returning home and said, son, today the Lord as corrected me. I told you no about that request because I cannot ersonally provide it for you. But I want you to know that I appreciate ou and the life you are living. You study hard and make good grades; ou work hard and you are respectful to your mother and me. I really do ant to know the desire of your heart and I want to bless that into your fe."

"We then knelt down in his room and spent some time in prayer." hen I said, "Son, I want to bless you with the words of my agreement. Matthew 18:19 says that God honors agreement. "The Lord bless you, on, with the desire of your heart today." "Within a few weeks, he had eceived that which he had desired. It proved to be a wonderful blessing his life."

### 7. The Meaning of Your Child's Name

Books are available which give the meaning of most names. But ou can also give your child a Christian name. Search the Scriptures to nd a Bible name which most accurately expresses the desires of your eart for your child. You can also research the meaning of your child's resent name. If the name given at birth expresses the desires of your eart, use it in your blessing ceremony. If it doesn't come up to your xpectations, use the new Christian name to describe his life. Then lease upon your child the full meaning and impact of that name, xpecting God to form those positive character traits in his life.

## PROGRAMING A SPECIAL BLESSING SERVICE

Your special blessing service for your child should be planne ahead of time so that all those you invite will have sufficient time prepare for the event. That should include:

- time for them to pray and fast if they so desire to prepare the hearts to impart blessings to your child.
- It would be well to ask them to read the book "Imparting Th Blessing" before they come for the blessing service.

They could either do it alone or you could meet weekly for several week to listen to the cassettes or cd's and review the study material. It important that those you invite understand the principles of blessin before they come to the special blessing service.

- They should also be prepared ahead of time with a blessin for your child. These should be written out.

Their attention should be directed toward the child receiving th blessing.

Now, here is a program to follow to prepare for the blessin service.

- Jewish families plan special blessing services over their sor at age 13 and daughters at age 12.
- Every member of your family should have a special blessin service, including mom and dad.
- For children, you need to prepare your child.
- Teach your child the principles given in these lessons.
- Study the Scriptures given in the lessons together so that h she will see how God has used the blessing in the Bible t bring His favor upon sons and daughters.
- Have your child prepare his/her own blessings which he/sh wants to speak over each member of the family and friend: His/Her blessing to them should be in the form of expression of appreciation for their influence in his/her life.

- Encourage your child to memorize favorite verses of Scripture to be quoted during the blessing service. He/She might like to select a poem which has been a favorite in life, or a hymn or chorus which has been encouraging to his/her life. A friend can be asked to sing the hymn. Do everything you can to prepare your child for a very special time in his or her life.

    Select your guests carefully. Make sure that they are ready so that they will not show up for the service unprepared. If they wish to bring a special gift to your child, let them do so.

- Plan your meal well ahead. Prepare a special meal, including some of the favorite dishes of your child. Let the child know that this meal is for him or her in their honor.

When you have completed the meal, leave the dishes to be cleaned later and move directly into the room where the blessing ceremony will take place.

When the ceremony begins:
- Welcome your guest and have prayer.
- Let your child begin with his Scripture and words of appreciation for each member of the family and for friends.
- Then have your child seated in the middle of the group.
- The parents should follow with the blessings they have prepared to speak over him.
- The other members of the family, brothers, sisters, and grandparents can speak their blessings.
- Let each of the friends who have prepared a blessing read it to him/her.
- Each person blessing should stand before the child while speaking.
- After the blessings, gather around your child, lay hands on him/her, allow time for prayer.
- If people bring gifts, let the child open them.
- Dismiss with prayer.

A Blessing to Model

It would be inappropriate to end this study without giving suggested model one can use for blessing children. Here is one Mr Ligon prepared for each of her sons before their special blessing servic The model used here was given to her younger son but the words wer similar for both except for the difference in the meaning of their names.

"To my beloved son, John Wesley Ligon. Your name means 'Th Beloved of God' (Luke 1:15-17, John 1:6-7). 'There was a man sent fror God whose name was John. The same came for a witness, to bear witnes of the Light that all men through him might believe.'" She went on t talk about how Scripture had meaning in his life. She referred to hi name, John, and the meaning of that name. She pointed out to him that h was named after the founder of the Methodist Church, John Wesley. Sh talked about the life and character of John the Baptist and John Wesley.

Then she moved into the blessing saying, "To my son of m womb and covenant before God and man, surely you fragrance, my sor is like the fragrance of a field which the Lord has blessed. Therefor may God give to you the dew of heaven, of the fatness of the earth, an plenty of grain and oil. Do not give your strength to women nor you ways to that which destroys covenant men. It is not good for men t drink wine and intoxicating drink lest they drink and forget the law an pervert the justice of all who are appointed to die. Open your mouth Judge righteously and plead the cause of the poor and needy. Open you mouth and preach that Gospel in the wisdom, knowledge and power c God. May you and your household always love God with all your hear Fear Him and reverence His Name, for out of the heart proceed the issue of life. May God bless you with a virtuous, God-fearing, wife who i beautiful in spirit, soul and body. May she be a person with a servar heart, a teacher in the love and admonition of the Lord, imparting speci grace to your children. May she extend her hand to the poor and need and may the law of kindness, gentleness and generosity be expresse from her heart. May your wife be blessed as Rachael and Leah, th builders of the household of faith and be like a fruitful vine in the heart c your home. May your children be as olive plants in the house of the Lor

...d as pillars sculptured in palace style and polished with the Spirit and ...lory of God. May the names of you and your family be written in the ...amb's Book of Life and may you be found with faith and faithfulness ...hen the Lord comes. May the zeal, the love and power of God always ...e evident in your life.

"The Lord bless you with good health and may God's angel go ...efore you and cause you to succeed. I say blessed are you because you ...ave made Jesus Christ your Lord and God. I love you dearly and bless ...ou with my life, love and prayers."    -Mother

Well, there is the blessing of a mother spoken over her son who is ...o precious to her. It was spoken over each of her sons in a special ...ervice for them. It was prepared after much meditation, prayer and ...asting. It was expected to be fulfilled, even if he were to go through a ...ifficult time during which it appeared that he was going to do just the ...pposite.

When you have worked through all the resources given in this ...esson, and you have begun your blessing ceremony, you can expect the ...rophetic Word of God to be expressed over your child. Then the ...nointing of the Holy Spirit will come upon him and he will receive ...lessing from God. May these teachings bless you and your children ...reatly.

# Quiz – Lesson 11

1. The child should be prepared ahead of time, before a blessing service to expect to receive something special from the _____

2. When Jesus blessed His disciples in Matthew 5, He was able to see _____ before they occurred.

3. Jesus always told His disciples you _____, not one day you will _____

4. Through God's promises, we partake of the _____ nature.

5. A special _____ service should be planned for each child.

*Answers found at end of workbook*

# Assignment - Lesson 11

1. Discuss a time to have a special blessing service for each member of your family. Birth days are always a possibility. Whatever the plans, do not do all of them at the same time. Do one at a time.

2. Commit yourselves to take time each day to speak blessing over each other - for the rest of your lives.

3. Prepare yourselves to have a group blessing service Next week as your last class together.

4. Have a great blessing journey!

# Blessing Service

## Celebration

Tonight is a time for celebration of the completion of the Father's Blessing Course. We congratulate you on your success. The eight weeks together have helped the families develop new habits to carry the family blessings forward in your homes on a daily basis.

Here is what your group is encouraged to do tonight:

1. Plan a covered dish meal together tonight to celebrate your graduation.

2. Following the meal, allow time for testimonies from family members on the benefits they have been experiencing because of the daily blessing.

3. One family at a time, place each family in the center of the room and impart blessing and success on them for their future.

4. Plan a follow-up meeting with the families who wish to move into leadership as Journeyman families and finally Torchbearers. They will commit to enlist new families and lead a group.

5. When you have time over the next couple of weeks please write a testimony telling what the Lord has done for you and your family through the practicing the principles of blessing. The testimony may be used in our publications or presentations. We will withhold the last name when used.

# Quiz Answers

## Lesson 2

1. The High Priestly blessing; 2. Irrevocable; 3. The Angel of the Lord; 4. Bless them; 5. Bless

## Lesson 3

1. Children; 2. Failing to impart the blessing to them; 3. Bless; 4. The blessing; 5. He blessed the people; 6. Bless

## Lesson 4

1. The Priestly blessing; 2. By speaking the blessing; 3. God; 4. The spoken word

## Lesson 5

1. The Blood Covenant (eating the Passover Lamb and placing it's blood on the doorpost of their home); 2. God; 3. B; 4. God; 5. True

## Lesson 6

1. Right; 2. Ephraim; 3. Right; 4. Jesus Christ; 5. The Life of Jesus, Jesus receives Calvary; 6. Rachael and Leah

## Lesson 7

1. Isaac, Abraham; 2. True

## Lesson 8

1. Older should serve the younger; 2. Rebekah; 3. Genesis 48; 4. Numbers 6:24-26

## Lesson 9

l. Sweet; 2. Visualize; 3. Potential; 4. Faith; 5. Discipline; 6. Verbal

## Lesson 10

1. Law and the malediction; 2. Curse; 3. Sweet, Bitter; 4. Curse; 5. Evil is the absence of good;

6. Punishment inflicts pain while discipline forms character

## Lesson 11

1. Lord; 2. Blessings; 3. Are, Become; 4. Divine; 5. Blessing

Pastor Bill &
Dorothy Jean Ligon

# The Father's Blessing

PO Box 2480
Brunswick, GA 31521

Phone: (912) 267-9140
Fax: (912) 262-6175

**thefathersblessing.com**

The website provides secure (SSL) ordering online.
Otherwise you may call or mail in your order.

# ORDER FORM

Date: _____

Book

4 CD Album

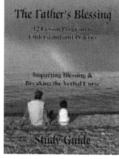
Group Study Book

Group Study 12 Lesson DVD Album

| How to release God's blessing on your family. | Materials | Price | Amt. | Total |
|---|---|---|---|---|
| Also, how to break the verbal curse. | Book & 4 CD Album | $ 38.00 | | |
| | Book | $ 8.00 | | |
| | 4 CD Album | $ 30.00 | | |
| Same Blessing Material Designed for Study Groups | Group Study Book - 12 Lesson | $ 12.00 | | |
| | Group Study 12 Lesson DVD's | $ 40.00 | | |

## Leadership Series

Biblical character traits necessary to raise up responsible leaders in the church and home.

## Anointing

Two Anointings.

One fades and one abides.

Learn about the anointing that abides.

## Maturi

Learn about stages of spi growth to m in Christ.

**Childh
Sonsh
Husband
Fatherh**

| **4 CD Albums** | Materials | Price | Amt. | Total |
|---|---|---|---|---|
| Teaching Series by | Steps to Maturity | $ 30.00 | | |
| | The Anointing | $ 30.00 | | |
| Pastor Bill Ligon | Leadership Series | $ 30.00 | | |
| | Faith Foundations | $ 30.00 | | |

## Children's Books Hard Cover

**Teaching the 10 Commandments**

**CD with all 10 Stories**

| Title | Price | Amt. | Total |
|---|---|---|---|
| 4th - Beaver Sunday | 14.95 | | |
| 7th - Skippy and Miss June | 14.95 | | |
| 8th - The Bee and The Bear | 12.95 | | |
| 9th - The One-O-Nine | 14.95 | | |
| 10 Commandments CD | 10.00 | | |

| gle CD's | Amt. | $ 7.00 per CD |
|---|---|---|
| eeming Your Children | | |
| Father's Faith | | |
| er, Build an Altar | | |
| Blessing it Really Works | | |
| urrection Life | | |
| Power of Obedience | | |
| Way of Restoration | | |
| ding the Blood of Jesus | | |
| 's Blessing on Your Health | | |
| t Her Honor | | |
| enant Blessings | | |

| Anointing Oil | Price | Amt. | Total |
|---|---|---|---|
| Altar Bottle | 30.00 | | |
| The Father's Faith | 5.00 | | |

| Total Items | | Total Amount - from all sections | |
|---|---|---|---|
| **Compute Shipping:** 1 = $5.00   2-6 = $8.00   7-12 = 12.00   13-20 = $20.00 <br> er 20 items = actual cost plus $10.00 handling | | | |
| cludes total + shipping   **Georgia Sales Tax** (Georgia Residents Only)  %7 | | | |
| **Grand Total** | | | |

lease Fill in all the Order Information - Check or Money Order (to: PO Box 2480 Brunswick, GA 31521)

me:_____ Phone:_____ Email:_____

dress:_____ City:_____ State:_____ Zip:_____

pe: M/C_____ Visa_____ Card Number:_____

p. Date:_____ CVV number (3 numbers on back of the card)_____

Made in the USA
Charleston, SC
29 April 2011